Anonymous

Hymns for the Use of the Sabbath School of the Second Reformed

Church, Albany, N.Y.

Anonymous

Hymns for the Use of the Sabbath School of the Second Reformed Church, Albany, N.Y.

ISBN/EAN: 9783337296407

Printed in Europe, USA, Canada, Australia, Japan

Cover: Foto ©Thomas Meinert / pixelio.de

More available books at **www.hansebooks.com**

HYMNS

FOR THE USE OF THE

SABBATH SCHOOL

OF THE

SECOND REFORMED CHURCH

ALBANY, N. Y.

ALBANY:
WEED, PARSONS & CO., PRINTERS,
1868.

THE HAPPY LAND.

[From the Happy Voices, page 1.]

There is a happy land,
   Far, far away,
Where saints in glory stand,
   Bright, bright as day.
Oh how they sweetly sing,
" Worthy is our Saviour King;"
Loud let his praises ring,
   Praise, praise for aye,

Come to that happy land,
   Come, come away.
Why will ye doubting stand,
   Why still delay?
Oh, we shall happy be,
When, from sin and sorrow free,
Lord. we shall dwell with thee,
   Blest, blest for aye.

Bright in that happy land,
   Beams every eye:
Kept by a Father,s hand,
   Love cannot die.
Oh then to glory run;
Be a crown and kingdom won;
And bright, above the sun,
   We'll reign for aye.

1

WONT YOU VOLUNTEER?

[From the Happy Voices, page 5.]

Come, boys, come, girls, wont you volunteer?
 If you'd reign in heaven above, you must battle here;
Say not, say not, we are weak and few;
 Only battle for the right, God will strengthen you.
  CHORUS.—March on, march on, singing as you go;
       March on, march on, do not fear the foe;
       March on, march on, singing as you go;
       March on, march on, do not fear the foe;

Come, boys, come, girls, wont you volunteer?
 Youthful soldiers of the cross, to our ranks repair;
List not, list not, to the world and sin,
 Turn away from foes without, and from foes within.
  CHORUS.—March on, march on, etc.

Come, boys, come, girls, wont you volunteer?
 Jesus bought you with his blood; how can you forbear?
Sinful, dying, to your help he flew,
 Wont you love and live for him who has died for you?
  CHORUS.—March on, march on, etc.

Come, boys, come, girls, wont you volunteer?
 Soon the vict'ry shall be yours, if you persevere;
Singing, shining, on a heavenly throne,
 You shall strike a harp of gold and wear a golden crown.
  CHORUS.—March on, march on, etc.

AROUND THE THRONE.

[From the Happy Voices, page 11.]

Around the throne of God in heaven,
 Thousands of children stand;
Children whose sins are all forgiven,
 A holy, happy band,
  Singing, glory, glory, glory be to God on high.

In flowing robes of spotless white
  See every one arrayed;
Dwelling in everlasting light,
  And joys that never fade,
    Singing, Glory, glory, glory, etc.

What brought them to that world above—
  That heaven so bright and fair,
Where all is peace and joy and love?
  How came those children there?
    Singing, Glory, glory, glory, etc.

Because the Saviour shed his blood
  To wash away their sin:
Bathed in that pure and precious flood,
  Behold them white and clean,
    Singing, Glory, glory, glory, etc.

On earth they sought the Saviour's grace,
  On earth they loved his name;
So now they see his blessed face,
  And stand before the Lamb,
    Singing, Glory, glory, glory, etc.

UNIVERSAL PRAISE.

[From the Happy Voices, page 12.]

The valleys and the mountains,
  The woodland and the plain,
The rivers and the fountains,
  The sunshine and the rain,
The stars that shine above me,
  The flowers that deck the sod,
Proclaim aloud the glory of my God.
  Praises, holy adoration,
Praises to the God above;
  Praises thro' the wide creation,
Sound aloud his greatness and his love.

And shall the voice of nature
   Thus glorify its King;
And man, the noble creature,
   No grateful tribute bring?
Shall mercy strew his pathway,
   And all the senses please,
And man withold the sacrifice of praise?
   Praise him, ye that live for ever;
Praise him every heart and voice:
   Praise him, he's the glorious giver;
Praise him in your sorrows and your joys

The word of life he gave us
   To guide us to the sky;
That he might justly save us,
   He sent his son to die—
To die in shame and anguish,
   To die a sacrifice;
To save us from the death that never dies
   Praise him, praise him for salvation;
Praise him, praise him for his son;
   Praise him, every tribe and nation;
Praise him for the battle he has won.

Then train your youthful voices
   To hymn his praise above;
For he who here rejoices
   In Jesus' dying love,
Around his throne in glory
   Shall all his love proclaim,
And sing the song of Moses and the lamb.
   Praise him, praise th' eternal Father;
Praise him, praise th' eternal Son:
   Praise him, praise the three together,
Father, Son, and Spirit, three in One.

TO THEE, MY GOD AND SAVIOUR.

[From the Happy Voices, page 13.]

To thee, my God and Saviour
  My heart exulting springs,
Rejoicing in thy favor,
  Almighty King of kings;
I'll celebrate thy glory
  With all the saints above,
And tell the wondrous story
  Of thy love.

CHORUS.

Glory, glory, hallelujah!
  Glory to the God of love;
Glory, glory. hallelujah!
  Glory ever be to God above.

Soon as the morn with roses
  Bedecks the dewy east,
And when the sun reposes
  Upon the ocean's breast,
My voice in supplication,
  Jehovah, thou shalt hear;
Oh grant me thy salvation,
  And draw near.
    Glory, glory, etc.

By thee, through life supported,
  I pass the dangerous road,
By heavenly hosts escorted
  Up to their bright abode;
There cast my crown before thee,
  My toils and conflicts o'er,
And gratefully adore thee
  Evermore.
    Glory, glory, etc.

HOSANNA.

[From the Happy Voices, page 14.]

What are those soul reviving strains
　Which echo thus from Salem's plains?
What anthems loud, and louder still,
　So sweetly sound from Zion's hill?
"Glory, glory!" let us sing,
　While heaven and earth with "Glory!" ring,
Hosanna, hosanna, hosanna to the Lamb of God!

Lo, 'tis an infant chorus sings
　"Hosanna to the King of kings!"
The Saviour comes, and babes proclaim
　Salvation sent in Jesus' name,
　　Glory, glory, etc.

Messiah's name shall joy impart,
　Alike to Jew and Gentile heart;
He bled for us, he bled for you,
　And we will sing Hosanna too.
　　Glory, glory, etc.

Proclaim Hosannas loud and clear.
　See David's Son and Lord appear;
All praise on earth to him be given,
　And "Glory!" shout through highest heaven.
　　Glory, glory, etc.

HALLELUJAH.

[From the Happy Voices, page 16.]

In the far better land of glory and light
The ransomed are singing in garments of white,
The harpers are harping, and all the bright train
Sing the song of redemption—"The Lamb that was slain."
　Hallelujah to the Lamb, Hallelujah to the Lamb,
　Hallelujah, Hallelujah, Hallelujah, Amen.

Hallelujah to the Lamb,
Hallelujah, Hallelujah, Hallelujah, Amen.

Like the sound of the sea swells their chorus of praise
Round the star-circled crown of the Ancient of days,
And thrones and dominions re-echo the strain
Of glory eternal to him that was slain.
Hallelujah to the Lamb etc.

Dear Saviour, may we, with our voices so faint,
Sing the chorus celestial with angel and saint?
Yes, yes, we will sing, and thine ear we will gain
With the song of redemption—"The Lamb that was slain."
Hallelujah to the Lamb, etc.

Now, children and teachers, and friends, all unite
In a loud hallelujah with the ransomed in light;
To Jesus we'll sing that melodius strain,
The song of redemption—"The Lamb that was slain."

COME AND JOIN THE ARMY.

[From the Happy Voices, page 18.]
We're marching to the camp above;
  Oh wont you come and join us?
We've shaken off the chains of sin,
  No longer they confine us.
    Then come and join the army,
    Then come and join the army;
      Oh gird the gospel armor on,
    And come and join the army.

We once as rebels boldly fought,
  The rebel banner o'er us,
But Jesus won us by his cross,
  And now leads on before us.
    Then come and join the army, etc.

And tho' against the shield of faith
  The fiery darts may rattle,

A soldier Jesus never lost,
  And never lost a battle.
    Then come and join the army, etc.

He'll give us peace and holy joy
  On this side of the river,
And when we've passed the swelling flood,
  Eternal life forever.
    Then come and join the army, etc.

And soon the conflict will be o'er,
  And will it not be glorious
To leave the battle-field for heaven,
  Rejoicing and victorious!
    Then come and join the army, etc.

I WANT TO BE AN ANGEL.

[From the Happy Voices, page 22.]

I want to be an angel,
  And with the angels stand,
A crown upon my forehead,
  A harp within my hand;
There, right before my Saviour,
  So glorious and so brtght,
I'd wake the sweetest music,
  And praise him day and night.

I never should be weary,
  Nor ever shed a tear,
Nor ever know a sorrow,
  Nor ever feel a fear;
But blessed, pure, and holy,
  I'd dwell in Jesus' sight,
And with ten thousand thousands
  Praise him both day and night.

I know I'm weak and sinful,
  But Jesus will forgive;

For many litle children
　　Have gone to heaven to live.
Dear Saviour, when I languish,
　　And lay me down to die,
Oh send a shining angel
　　To bear me to the sky.

Oh there I'll be an angel,
　　And with the angels stand,
A crown upon my forehead,
　　A harp within my hand;
And there before my Saviour,
　　So glorious and so bright,
I'll join the heavenly music,
　　And praise him day and night.

THE SOLID ROCK.

[From the Golden Censer, page 83.]

My hope is built on nothing less
Than Jesus' blood and righteousness;
I dare not trust the sweetest frame,
But wholly lean on Jesus' name:
　　On Christ, the solid rock I stand;
　　All other ground is sinking sand,
　　All other ground is sinking sand.

When darkness seems to veil his face,
I rest on his unchanging grace;
In every high and stormy gale,
My anchor holds within the vale.
　　On Christ, the solid rock, etc.

His oath, his covenant, and blood,
Support me in the 'whelming flood;
When all around my soul gives way,
He then is all my hope and stay.
　　On Christ, the solid rock, etc.

SINGING OF JESUS.

[From the Happy Voices, page 22.]

Come, let us sing of Jesus,
  While hearts and accents blend,
Come, let us sing of Jesus,
  The sinner's only friend,
His holy soul rejoices
  Amid the choirs above,
To hear our youthful voices
  Exulting in his love.

We love to sing of Jesus,
  Who wept our path along;
We love to sing of Jesus,
  The tempted and the strong;
None who besought his healing,
  He passed unheeded by;
And still retains his feeling
  For us above the sky.

We love to sing of Jesus,
  Who died our souls to save;
We love to sing of Jesus,
  Triumphant o'er the grave;
And in our hour of danger
  We'll trust his love alone,
Who once slept in a manger,
  And now sits on the throne.

Then let us sing of Jesus,
  While yet on earth we stay,
And hope to sing of Jesus
  Throughout eternal day;
For those who here confess him
  He will in heaven confess,
And faithful hearts that bless him
  He will forever bless

LONELY TRAVELER.

[From the Golden Chain, page 66.]

I 'm a lonely traveler here,
    Weary, oppressed,
But my journey's end is near—
    Soon shall I rest !
Dark and dreary is the way,
    Toiling I 've come ;
Ask me not with you to stay,
    Yonder's my home.

I 'm a weary traveler here,
    I must go on,
For my journey's end is near,
    I must be gone.
Brighter joys than earth can give,
    Win me away ;
Pleasures that forever live—
    I can not stay.

I 'm a traveler to a land
    Where all is fair,
Where is seen no broken band—
    All, all are there.
Where no tear shall ever fall,
    Nor heart be sad ;
Where the glory is for all,
    And all are glad.

I 'm a traveler, and I go
    Where all is fair ;
Farewell, all I 've loved below—
    I must be there.
Worldly honors, hopes, and gain,
    All I resign ;
Welcome sorrow, grief, and pain,
    If heaven be mine.

I 'm a traveler—call me not—
    Upward my way;
Yonder is my rest and lot;
    I can not stay.
Farewell, earthly pleasures all,
    Pilgrim I 'll roam;
Hail me not—in vain you call
    Yonder's my home.

THE RIVER OF LIFE.

[From the Golden Chain, page 67.]

Oh! there is a river whose fresh waters flow
O'er earth's broadest surface, a cure for all woe:
Its streams are all healing, there's life in each wave,
Oh, try it and prove it, 'tis mighty to save.
    Jesus calls, will you come? will you come? will you
        come? will you come?
    Jesus calls, will you come? will you come?
    Come to Jesus, come now,
    Yes, come, O come to Jesus,
    Come to Jesus, come now,
    Yes, come, O come to Jesus,
    Come to Jesus, come now.

Oh! drink of this river, its full crystal flood
Refreshes and lightens of sin's weary load;
Its ripples ne'er mix with the billows of strife,
This is the "Pure River of Water of Life."
    Jesus calls, etc.

This beautiful river our boast well may be,
'Tis fresh, overflowing, and better, 'tis free!
The sin-sick rejoice in this "peace-speaking" tide,
This river is Jesus, the "once crucified."
    Jesus calls, etc.

REST FOR THE WEARY.

[From the Golden Chain, page 36.]

In the Christian's home in glory,
    There remains a land of rest,
There my Saviour's gone before me,
    To fulfill my soul's request; .
      There is rest for the weary,
      There is rest for the weary,
      There is rest for the weary,
      There is rest for you—
      On the other side of Jordan,
      In the sweet fields of Eden,
      Where the tree of life is blooming,
      There is rest for you.

He is fitting up my mansion,
    Which eternally shall stand,
For my stay shall not be transient
    In that holy, happy land.
      There is rest, etc.

Pain nor sickness ne'er shall enter,
    Grief nor woe my lot shall share;
But in that celestial center,
    I a crown of life shall wear.
      There is rest, etc.

Death itself shall then be vanquished,
    And his sting shall be withdrawn;
Shout for gladness, O ye ransomed,
    Hail with joy the rising morn.
      There is rest, etc.

Sing, O sing, ye heirs of glory;
    Shout your triumph as you go;
Zion's gates will open for you,
    You shall find an entrance through.
      There is rest, etc.

THE SUNDAY-SCHOOL ARMY.

[From the Golden Chain, page 27.]

O, do not be discouraged,
  For Jesus is your Friend,
O, do not be discouraged,
  For Jesus is your Friend.
He will give you grace to conquer,
He will give you grace to conquer,
  And keep you to the end.
    I am glad I'm in this army,
      Yes, I'm glad I'm in this army,
    Yes, I'm glad I'm in this army,
      And I'll battle for the school.

Fight on, ye little soldiers,
  The battle you shall win;
Fight on, ye little soldiers,
  The battle you shall win.
For the Saviour is your Captain,
For the Saviour is your Captain,
  And he has vanquished sin.—*Chorus.*

And when the conflict's over,
  Before him you shall stand;
And when the conflict's over,
  Before him you shall stand.
You shall sing his praise for ever,
You shall sing his praise for ever,
  In Canaan's happy land.—*Chorus.*

THE BEST DAY OF ALL THE WEEK.

[From the Golden Shower, page 4.]

O what beauties adorn the bright Sabbath morn,
  The best day of all the week,
And how gladly we start with a light, happy heart,
  As the house of the Lord we seek.

Humbly let us enter in,
Praying to be free from sin,
Pure without and pure within,
   On this Sabbath day.
Let us keep, well keep this blessed Sabbath day,
This holy Sabbath day, this holy Sabbath day,
Let us keep, well keep this holy Sabbath day,
'Tis the best day of all the week.

Be it ever our care in that place of prayer,
  Our spirits above to raise;
Let us try to drive out each vain worldly thought,
  From God's holy courts of praise;
    Let no folly there intrude,
    Naught to mar our tranquil mood,
    Naught but what is true and good,
     On this Sabbath day.
       Let us keep, well keep, &c.,

And our joy is full when the dear Sabbath school,
  Throws open its friendly door;
For we're sure there to find our teachers so kind
  With riches of sacred lore.
    As our voices all we raise
    In sweet songs of love and praise,
    May we tread in wisdom's ways,
     On this Sabbath day.
       Let us keep, well keep, &c.,

And when we go back to our week-day track,
  Our lessons, and work, and play;
Let us hold ever dear the counsels we hear,
  On the holy Sabbath day.
    And remember that God's eye
    Ever watches from on high,
    And each day he is as nigh,
     As the Sabbath day.
       Let us keep, well keep, &c.

CALL THE CHILDREN EARLY.

[From the Golden Chain, page 30.]

Call the children early, mother,
    While the birds do sing;
While the dew is on the flowers,
    Which by the hill side spring,
Oft repeat the waking word,
    Till they rise to praise the Lord,
Oft repeat the waking word,
    Till they rise to praise the Lord.

Call the children early, father,
    While the dew is on;
Great the work that must be done
    Before the morning's gone.
Call them round the altar bright
    On which burns devotion's light,
Call them round the altar bright,
    On which burns devotion's light.

Call the children early, teacher—
    To their wondering eyes,
Every Sabbath day, set forth
    The pearl of richest price.
Call them early to the Lord—
    Thou shalt reap a rich reward,
Call them early to the Lord,
    Thou shalt reap a rich reward.

Call the children early, Shepherd,
    Give the lambs thy care;
See that they are folded safe
    Within the house of prayer.
Call them at the dawn of day,
    Lead them in the narrow way,
Call them at the dawn of day,
    Lead them in the narrow way.

SHALL WE SING IN HEAVEN?

[From the Golden Chain, page 34.]

Shall we sing in heaven forever—
    Shall we sing? Shall we sing?
Shall we sing in heaven forever
    In that happy land?
Yes! oh, yes! in that land, that happy land,
    They that meet shall sing forever,
    Far beyond the rolling river,
    Meet to sing, and love forever
    In that happy land.

Shall we know each other ever
    In that land? In that land?
Shall we know each other ever
    In that happy land?
Yes! oh, yes! in that land, that happy land,
    They that meet shall know each other,
    Far beyond, etc.

Shall we sing with holy angels
    In that land?
Shall we sing with holy angels
    In that happy land?
Yes! oh, yes! in that land, that happy land,
    Saints and angels sing forever
    Far beyond the rolling river,
    Meet to sing, and love forever
    In that happy land!

Shall we meet our faithful teachers
    In that land?
Shall we meet our faithful teachers
    In that happy land?
Yes! oh, yes! in that land, that happy land,
    Teachers and scholars meet together,
    Far beyond the rolling river, etc.

2

Shall we know our blessed Saviour
In that land?
Shall we know our blessed Saviour
In that happy land?
Yes! oh, yes! in that land, that happy land,
We shall know our blessed Saviour
Far beyond the rolling river,
Love and serve him there forever,
In that happy land!

ON A SUNDAY MORNING.

[From the Golden Shower, page 6.]

Children, can you truly tell,
Do you know the story well,
Every girl and every boy,
Why the angels sing for joy,
On a Sunday morning,
On a Sunday morning,
On a Sunday morning,
The angels sing for joy.

Yes, we know the story well,
Listen now, and hear us tell,
Every girl and every boy,
Why the angels sing for joy,
On a Sunday morning, &c.

Angels rolled the rock away,
Death gave up his mighty prey,
Jesus triumphed o'er the tomb,
Rising with immortal bloom,
On a Sunday morning.

Lift ye saints, lift up your eyes,
Now to glory see him rise;
Hosts of angels on the road,
Hail and sing th 'incarnate God,
On a Sunday morning.

Vain the stone, the watch, the seal,
Jesus burst the gates of hell;
Death in vain forbids his rise,
Jesus opened Paradise
    On a Sunday morning.

"Peace," our every heart shall fill,
"Peace on earth, to men good will;"
We will join the angel's song,
And the pleasant notes prolong
    On a Sunday morning.

THE ROYAL PROCLAMATION.
[From the Golden Chain, page 40.]

Hear the royal proclamation,
The glad tidings of salvation,
Publishing to every creature,
To the ruined sons of nature:
    Jesus reigns, Jesus reigns, Jesus reigns,
    Jesus reigns, he reigns victorious,
    Over heaven and earth most glorious,
    Jesus reigns, Jesus reigns, Jesus reigns!

See the royal banner flying,
Hear the heralds loudly crying,
"Rebel sinners, royal favor,
Now is offered by the Saviour."
    Jesus reigns, etc.

"Here is wine, and milk, and honey;
Come, and purchase without money;
Mercy flowing from a fountain,
Streaming from the holy mountain."
    Jesus reigns, etc.

Shout, ye tongues of every nation,
To the bounds of the creation;

Shout the praise of Judah's Lion,
The Almighty Prince of Zion.
  Jesus reigns, etc.

Shout, ye saints, make joyful mention,
Christ hath purchased our redemption,
Angels, shout the pleasing story,
Through the brighter worlds of glory.
  Jesus reigns, etc.

THE PRECIOUS STORY.

[From the Happy Voices, page 22.]

How precious is the story
  Of our Redeemer's birth,
Who left the realms of glory,
  And came to dwell on earth;
He saw our sad condition,
  Our guilt and sin and shame;
To save us from perdition
  The blessed Jesus came.

He came to earth from heaven,
  To weep and bleed and die,
That we might be forgiven,
  And raised to God on high.
His kindness and compassion
  To children then were shown,
The heirs of his salvation,
  He claimed them for his own.

Oh may I love this Saviour,
  So good, so kind, so mild;
And may I find his favor,
  A young, though sinful child;
And in his blessed heaven,
  May I at last appear,
With all my sins forgiven,
  To know and praise him there.

THE SWEETEST NAME.

[From the Golden Censer, page 13.]

There is no name so sweet on earth,
No name so sweet in heaven.
The name before his wondrous birth
To Christ. the Saviour given.
We love to sing around our **King**,
And hail him blessed Jesus;
For there's no word ever heard,
So dear, so sweet, as Jesus.

His human name they did proclaim,
When Abram's son they seal'd him:
The name that still by God's good will,
Deliverer revealed him.
We love to sing, etc.

And when he hung upon the tree,
They wrote his name above him,
That all might see the reason we
For evermore must love him.
We love to sing, etc.

So now upon his Father's throne,
Almighty to release us
From sin and pains, he gladly reigns,
The Prince and Saviour, Jesus.
We love to sing, etc.

DARE TO DO RIGHT! DARE TO BE TRUE!

[From the Golden Censer, page 8.]

Dare to do right! dare to be true!
You have a work that no other can do,
Do it so bravely. so kindly, so well,
Angels will hasten the story to tell.
Dare, dare to do right!
Dare, dare, dare to be true!
Dare to be true! dare to be true!

Dare to do right! dare to be true!
Other men's failures can never save you!
Stand by your conscience, your honor, your faith;
Stand like a hero, and battle till death.
  Dare to do right, etc.

Dare to do right! dare to be true!
God, who created you, cares for you too;
Treasures the tears that his striving ones shed,
Counts and protects every hair of your head.
  Dare to do right, etc.

Dare to do right! dare to be true!
Keep the great judgment-seat always in view;
Look at your work as you'll look at it then—
Scanned by Jehovah, and angels, and men.
  Dare to do right, etc.

Dare to do right! dare to be true!
Jesus, your Saviour, will carry you through;
City, and mansion, and throne all in sight,
Can you not dare to be true and do right?
  Dare to do right, etc.

JESUS PAID IT ALL.

[From the Golden Censer, page 12.]
Nothing, either great or small,
  Remains for me to do;
Jesus died, and paid it all,—
  Yes all the debt I owe.
   Jesus paid it all,
    All the debt I owe,
   Jesus died and paid it all,
    Yes, all the debt I owe.

When he from his lofty throne,
  Stoop'd down to do and die,
Everything was fully done;
  " 'Tis finished!" was his cry.
   Jesus paid it all, etc.

Weary, working, plodding one,
　Oh, wherefore toil you so?
Cease your doing—all was done;
　Yes, ages long ago.
　　　Jesus paid it all, etc.

Till to Jesus' work you cling,
　Alone by simple faith,
"Doing" is a deadly thing,
　Your "doing" ends in death.
　　　Jesus paid it all, etc.

Cast your deadly "doing" down,
　Down all at Jesus' feet;
Stand in Him, in Him alone,
　All glorious and complete.
　　　Jesus paid it all, etc.

ONE DAY NEARER HOME.

[From the Golden Shower, page 21.]

　　A crown of glory blight,
　　　By faith's clear eyes I see
　　In yonder realms of light
　　　Prepared for me.
I'm nearer my home, nearer my home, nearer my home
　　to-day;
Yes! nearer my home in heaven to-day,
Than ever I've been before.

　　O may I faithful prove,
　　　And keep the crown in view,
　　And thro' the storms of life
　　　My way pursue.

　　Jesus, be thou my guide,
　　　And all my steps attend,
　　O keep me near thy side,
　　　Be thou my friend.

Be thou my shield and sun,
My Saviour and my guard;
And when my work is done
My great reward.

THE COOLING SPRING.

[From the Golden Censer, page 47.]

O, a goodly thing is the cooling spring,
By the rock where the moss doth grow;
There is health in the tide. and there's music beside,
In the brooklet's bounding flow.
Merry, merry, little spring,
Sparkle on, sparkle on,
Merry, merry. little spring,
Sparkle on for me.

And as pure as heaven is the water given,
And its stream is forever new;
'Tis distilled in the sky. and it drops from on high,
In the showers and gentle dew.
Ripple, ripple, silv'ry brook,
Ripple on, ripple on,
Ripple, ripple. silv'ry brook,
Ripple on for me.

Let them say 'tis weak, but it's strength I'll seek,
And rejoice while I own its sway;
For its murmur to me is the echo of glee,
And it laughs as it bounds away.
Merry, merry, little spring, etc.

O, I love to drink from the foaming brink,
Of the bubbling, the cooling spring;
For the bright drops that shine more refreshing than
wine,
And its praise, its praise, we'll sing.
Merry, merry, little spring, etc.

THE BETTER LAND.

[From the Golden Chain, page 78.]

BOYS. Whither pilgrims are you going,
    Going each with staff in hand?
GIRLS. We are going on a journey,
    Going at our King's command.
ALL. Over hills, and plains, and valleys,
    We are going to his palace,
    We are going to his palace,
    Going to the better land;
    We are going to his palace,
    Going to the better land.

BOYS. Fear ye not the way so lonely,
    You, a little feeble band?
GIRLS. No, for friends, unseen, are near us,
    Holy angels round us stand.
ALL. Christ, our leader, walks beside us,
    He will guard and he will guide us,
    He will guard and he will guide us,
    Guide us to that better land:
    He will guard and he will guide us,
    Guide us to that better land.

BOYS. Tell me pilgrims, what you hope for
    In that far-off, better land?
GIRLS. Spotless robes and crowns of glory
    From a Saviour's loving hand.
ALL. We shall drink of life's clear river,
    We shall dwell with God for ever,
    We shall dwell with God for ever,
    In that bright, that better land.

BOYS. Pilgrims, may we travel with you
    To that bright and better land?
GIRLS. Come and welcome, come and welcome,
    Welcome to our pilgrim band.

ALL. Come, oh come, and do not leave us,
Christ is waiting to receive us,
Christ is waiting to receive us,
    In that bright, that better land.

"SEEKING JESUS."

[From the Golden Censer, page 68.]

Thro' the world we daily roam,
    Seeking Jesus, seeking Jesus;
None in vain for this have come,
    Seeking Jesus, seeking Jesus;
In all places high or lowly,
'Mid the sinful and the holy,
    Seeking Jesus, seeking Jesus.
        We shall find Him,
        We shall find Him,
        We shall find Him, if we seek,
        He will hear us when we speak;
        He will answer us in love,
        Take us home to dwell above.

If our days on earth are spent
    Seeking Jesus,
With all things we'll be content,
    Seeking Jesus:
Though our path be lone and dreary,
Though our steps be slow and weary,
    Seeking Jesus,
        We shall find Him, etc.

Soon our life will all be o'er,
    Seeking Jesus,
We shall reach the better shore,
    Seeking Jesus.
In that land of peace and pleasure,
We've laid up our dearest treasure,
    Seeking Jesus.
        We shall find Him, etc.

AUTUMN.

[From the Golden Chain, page 81.]

Holy Father, thou hast taught me,
    I should live to thee alone;
Year by year, thy hand hath brought me
    On thro' dangers oft unknown.
When I wandered, thou hast found me;
    When I doubted, sent me light,
Still thine arm has been around me,
    All my paths were in thy sight.

In the world will foes assail me,
    Craftier, stronger far than I;
And the strife may never fail me,
    Well I know before I die.
Therefore, Lord, I come, believing
    Thou canst give the power I need;
Thro' the prayer of faith receiving
    Strength—the spirit's strength, indeed.

I would trust in thy protecting,
    Wholly rest upon thine arm;
Follow wholly thy directing,
    Thou, mine only guard from harm!
Keep me from mine own undoing,
    Help me turn to thee when tried,
Still my footsteps, Father, viewing,
    Keep me ever at thy side.

THE GOSPEL SHIP.

[From the Golden Censer, page 52.]

The gospel ship is sailing,
    Sailing, sailing,
The gospel ship is sailing,
Bound for Canaan's happy shore;
All who would ship for glory,
    Glory, glory,

All who would ship for glory,
Come and welcome. rich and poor!
    Glory. hallelujah!
  All on board are sweetly singing,
    Glory, hallelujah!
  Hallelujah to the Lamb!

She has landed many thousands,
    Thousands, thousands,
She has landed many thousands,
On fair Canaan's happy shore;
And thousands now are sailing,
    Sailing, sailing,
And thousands now are sailing,
Yet there's room for thousands more.
    Glory, hallelujah, etc.

Sails filled with heavenly breezes,
    Breezes, breezes,
Sails filled with heavenly breezes,
Swiftly glides the ship along,
Her company are singing,
    Singing, singing,
Her company are singing,
Glory, glory is their song.
    Glory. hallelujah, etc.

Take passage now for glory,
    Glory. glory,
Take passage now for glory,
Sailing o'er life's troubled sea;
With us you shall be happy,
    Happy, happy,
With us you shall be happy,
Happy through eternity.
    Glory, hallelujah, etc.

I'LL RISE UP EARLY IN THE MORNING.

[From the Golden Chain, page 31.]

I 'll rise up early in the morning,
    The morning of the Sabbath day,
I 'll rise up early in the morning,
    And haste to Sabbath-school away.
For oh, I love the Sabbath-school,
The Sabbath-school, the Sabbath-school,
For oh, I love the Sabbath-school,
    The precious Sabbath-school.

While there I 'll listen to my teacher,
    And treasure up what he may say,
While there I 'll listen to my teacher,
    As up to heaven he points the way.
For oh, I love my teacher dear,
My teacher dear, my teacher dear:
For oh, I love my teacher dear,
    So good and kind to me.

I 'll learn my lesson in the Bible,
    And try to practice what I learn;
I 'll learn my lesson in the Bible,
    And every sinful way will shun.
For oh, I love that blessed book,
That blessed book, that blessed book,
For oh, I love that blessed book,
    So full of grace and truth.

Then I 'll not trifle any longer,
    Nor throw my precious hours away,
Then I 'll not trifle any longer,
    But go to Christ without delay;
And dwell with him in heaven above,
In heaven above, in heaven above—
And dwell with him in heaven above,
    A heaven of joy and love.

A SAVIOUR EVER NEAR.

[From the Golden Shower, page 26.]

Hush'd be my murmurings, let cares depart,
Jesus is near me, to cheer my heart;
He's near to help me whilst life's hours remain,
He speaks to cheer me in toil and in pain,
He speaks to cheer me in toil and in pain.
  Gentle angels near me glide,
  Hopes of glory 'round me 'bide,
  And there lingers by my side a Saviour, a Saviour,
    a Saviour ever near,
  A Saviour, a Saviour, a Saviour ever near.

Why should I languish—why should I fear?
In sorrow and anguish He's ever near;
Sleeping or waking—in pleasure or pain,
Roaming or resting, He'll near me remain.
    Gentle angels, etc.

Scenes that will vanish smile on me now,
Joys of a moment play round my brow,
But soon in heaven He'll meet me again,
There'll end my sorrow, and there'll end my pain,
    Gentle angels, etc.

MY SABBATH SONG.

[From the Golden Censer, page 6.]

Strains of music often greet me,
  As I join the busy throng,
But there's nothing half so pleasant,
  As the holy Sabbath song.
        No fear of ill,
        No fear of wrong,
     While I can sing my Sabbath song;
       My Sabbath song,
       My Sabbath song;
    I love to sing my Sabbath song.

'Tis a song of love and mercy
  Speaking peace to all mankind;
Telling sinners, poor and needy,
  Where the Saviour they may find.
      No fear of ill, etc.

Angels sweetly sing in glory
  Songs of praise to God, their King;
But the song of blest redemption
  Man, redeemed, alone can sing.
      No fear of ill, etc.

While I live, O, may I ever
  Love the holy Sabbath song;
And when death shall call me homeward,
  Join it with the blood-bought throng.
      No fear of ill, etc.

"SWEET LAND OF REST."

[From the Golden Censer, page 13.]

Sweet land of rest! for thee I sigh,
  When will the moment come?
When I shall lay my armor by,
  And dwell with Christ at home.
        Home, home, sweet, sweet home,
          And dwell with Christ at home.
        Home, home, sweet, sweet home,
          This world is not my home.

No tranquil joys on earth I know,
  No peaceful sheltering home—
The world's a wilderness of woe,
  This world is not my home.
        Home, home, etc.

To Jesus Christ I sought for rest,
  He bade me cease to roam,
But fly for succor to his breast,
  And he'd conduct me home.
        Home, home, etc.

Weary of wandering round and round
  This vale of sin and gloom,
I long to leave the unhallowed ground,
  And dwell with Christ at home.
      Home, home, etc.

WHITE ROBES.

[From the Golden Censer, page 84.]

Who are these in bright array,
  This exulting, happy throng,
Round the altar night and day,
  Singing one triumphant song?
      They have clean robes, white robes,
      White robes are waiting for me!
      Yes, clean robes, white robes,
      Wash'd in the blood of the Lamb!

These thro' fiery trials trod,
  These from great afflictions came;
Now before the throne of God,
  Sealed with his almighty name.
      They have clean robes, etc.

Clad in raiment pure and white,
  Victor palms in ev'ry hand.
Through their great Redeemer's might,
  More than conquerors they stand.
      They have clean robes, etc.

Joy and gladness banish sighs;
  Perfect love dispels all fears;
And forever from their eyes
  God shall wipe away their tears.
      They have clean robes, etc.

SWEETLY SING, SWEETLY SING.

[From the Golden Chain, page 70.]

Sweetly sing, sweetly sing,
Praises to our heavenly King;
Let us raise, let us raise
High our notes of praise;
Praise to Him whose name is Love,
Praise to Him who reigns above;
Raise your songs, raise your songs,
Now with thankful tongues.

Angels bright, angels bright,
Robed in garments pure and white,
Chant his praise, chant his praise,
In melodious lays:
But from that bright, happy throng,
Ne'er can come this sweetest song—
Redeeming love, redeeming love,
Brought us here above.

Far away, far away.
We in sin's dark valley lay,
Jesus came, Jesus came,
Blessed be his name!
He redeemed us by his grace,
Then prepared in heaven a place
To receive—to receive
All who will believe.

Now we know—now we know
We from heaven must shortly go:
Soon the call—soon the call
Comes to one and all.
Saviour! when *our* time shall come,
Take us to our heavenly home,
There we'll raise notes of praise,
Through unending days.

3

THE EVERGREEN SHORE.

[From the Golden Chain, page 76.]

We are joyously voyaging over the main,
    Bound for the evergreen shore,
Whose inhabitants never of sickness complain,
    And never see death any more.
  Then let the hurricane roar, roar,
  It will the sooner be o'er ;
  We will weather the blast, and will land at last,
  Safe on the evergreen shore.

We have nothing to fear from the wind and the wave,
    Under our Saviour's command ;
And our hearts in the midst of the dangers are brave ;
    For Jesus will bring us to land.
  Then let the, etc.

Both the winds and the waves our Commander controls ;
    Nothing can baffle his skill :
And his voice when the thundering hurricane rolls,
    Can make the loud tempest be still.
  Then let the, etc.

In the thick murky night, when the stars and the moon,
    Send not a glimmering ray,
Then the light of his countenance, brighter than noon,
    Will drive all our terror away.
  Then let the, etc.

Let the high heaving billow and mountainous wave,
    Fearfully overhead break ;
There is one by our side that can comfort and save ;—
    There 's one who will never forsake.
  Then let the, etc.

Let the vessel be wrecked on the rock, or the shoal,
    Sink to be seen never more ;
He will bear, none the less, every passenger soul,
    Safe, safe to the evergreen shore.
  Then let the, etc.

WE'RE NEARER HOME.

[From the Golden Shower, page 30.]

We know not what's before us,
    What trials are to come:
But each day passing o'er us,
    Brings us still nearer home.
We're nearer, nearer home,
    Our blessed, happy home,
Where grief and sin can never come,
    We're nearer, nearer home.
        Nearer home, nearer home,
        Nearer to my happy home,
        Nearer home, nearer home,
        Our blessed, happy home.

Tho' dark our path, and lonely,
    And clouds our sky o'ercast,
Let us remember only,
    That it will soon be passed.
        We're nearer, etc.

Whate'er of gloom or anguish
    Life to our hearts may bring,
In doubt we will not languish,
    But cheerfully we'll sing.
        We're nearer, etc.

"GLORY, GLORY TO THE LAMB."

[From the Golden Censer, page 4.]

Hark! the sweetest notes of angels singing,
    Glory, glory to the Lamb,
All the hosts of heaven their tribute bringing,
    Raising high the Saviour's name.
        We will join the beautiful angels,
        We will join the beautiful angels,
        Singing away, singing away,
        Glory, glory to the Lamb.

Ye for whom his precious life was given,
  Sacred themes to you belong;
Come. and join the glorious choir of heaven,
  Join the everlasting song.
      We will join, etc.

Hearts all filled with holy emulation,
  We unite with those above;
Sweet the theme—the theme of free salvation,
  Founts of everlasting love.
      We will join, &c.

Endless life in Christ our Lord possessing,
  Let us praise his precious name:
Glory, honor, riches, power, and blessing
  Be forever to the Lamb.
      We will join, etc.

I WILL BE GOOD, DEAR MOTHER.

[From the Golden Chain, page 74.]

"I will be good, dear mother,"
  I heard a sweet child say;
"I will be good—now watch me—
  I will be good all day."
She lifted up her bright young eyes
  With a soft and pleasing smile,
Then a mother's kiss was on her lip,
  So pure and free from guile.
    "I will be good, I will be good,
      I will be good to-day,
    I will be good, I will be good,
     . I will be good to-day.

And when night came, that little one,
  In kneeling down to pray,
Said in a soft and whisp'ring tone,
  " Have I been good to-day? "

O many, many bitter tears
　"Twould save us did we say,
Like that dear child, with earnest heart,
　"I will be good to-day."
　　I will be good, etc,

Jesus can help us to be good—
　To Him we'll humbly pray;
His grace alone can make us good,
　And keep us good all day.
He'll help us hate all evil thoughts,
　All sinful words and ways;
And in his service take delight,
　Thro' all our earthly days.
　　I will be good, etc.

SOMETHING TO DO IN HEAVEN.
[From the Golden Censer, page 80.]

There'll be something in heaven for children to do;
　None are idle in that blessed land.
There'll be loves for the hearts, there'll be thoughts for the
　mind,
And employment for each little hand.
　　　There'll be something to do;
　　　There'll be something to do;
　　　There'll be something for children to do;
　On the bright shining shore, where there's joy evermore,
　　　There'll be something for children to do.

There'll be lessons to learn of the wisdom of God,
　As they wander the green meadows o'er;
And they'll have for their teachers in that blest abode,
　All the good that have gone there before.
　　　There'll be something to do, etc.

There'll be errands of love from the mansions above,
　To the dear ones that linger below;
And it may be our Father the children will send
　To be angels of mercy in woe.
　　　There'll be something to do, etc.

CLIMBING UP ZION'S HILL.

[From the Golden Censer page 44.]

"I'm tryiug to climb up Zion's hill,"
  For the Saviour whispers "Love me;"
Tho' all beneath is dark as death,
  Yet the stars are bright above me.
        Then upward still,
        To Zion's hill,
    To the land of joy and beauty,
        My path before,
        Shines more and more,
    As it nears the golden city.
              I'm climbing up Zion's hill,
              I'm climbing up Zion's hill,
          Climbing, climbing, climbing up Zion's hill.

I know I'm but a little child,
  My strength will not protect me;
But then I am the Saviour's lamb,
  And he will uot neglect me.
        Then all the time
        I'll try to climb
    This holy hill of Zion:
        For I am sure,
        The way is pure,
    And on it comes "no lion."
              I'm climbing up, etc.

Then come with me, we'll upward go,
  And climb this hill together;
And as we walk, we'll sweetly talk,
  And sing as we go thither.
        Then mount up still
        God's holy hill,
    Till we reach the pearly portals;
        Where raptured tougues
        Proclaim the songs
  Of the shining-robed immortals.
              I'm climbing up, etc.

THE SUNDAY-SCHOOL.

[From the Golden Chain, page 4.]

The Sunday-school, that blessed place,
　Oh! I would rather stay
Within its walls a child of grace,
　Than spend my hours in play—
　　The Sunday-school, the Sunday-school,
　　　Oh! 'tis the place I love,
　　For there I learn the golden rule
　　　Which leads to joys above.

'Tis there I learn that Jesus died
　For sinners such as I;
Oh! what has all the world beside,
　That I should prize so high—
　　The Sunday-school, etc.

Then let our grateful tribute rise,
　And songs of praise be given
To Him who dwells above the skies,
　For such a blessing given—
　　The Sunday-school, etc.

And welcome then the Sunday-school,
　We'll read, and sing, and pray
That we may keep the golden rule,
　And never from it stray—
　　The Sunday-school, etc.

"EVEN ME."

[From the Golden Shower, page 83.]

Lord, I hear of show'rs of blessings,
　Thou art scattering full and free.
Show'rs the thirsty land refreshing,
　Let some droppings fall on me.
　　　Even me, even me,
　　　Let some droppings fall on me.

Pass me not, O God, my Father,
  Sinful though my heart may be;
Thou might'st leave me, but the rather
  Let thy mercy light on me,—
    Even me.

Pass me not, O gracious Saviour
  Let me live and cling to thee:
Fain I'm longing for thy favor,
  Whilst thou'rt calling, call for me—
    Even me.

Pass me not, O mighty Spirit,
  Thou canst make the blind to see:
Witnesses of Jesus' merit,
  Speak the word of power to me—
    Even me.

Love of God. so pure and changeless:
  Blood of Christ, so rich and free;
Grace of God, so rich and boundless,
  Magnify it all in me—
    Even me.

Pass me not, thy lost one bringing;
  Bind my heart, O Lord, to thee;
Whilst the streams of life are springing
  Blessing others, oh, bless me—
    Even me.

BEAUTIFUL ZION.

[From the Golden Shower, page 86.]
Beautiful Zion, built above,
Beautiful city that I love,
Beautiful gates of pearly white,
Beautiful temple—God its light.
  Beautiful gates of pearly white,
  Beautiful temple—God its light.

Beautiful heaven, where all is light,
Beautiful angels, clothed in white,
Beautiful strains, that never tire,
Beautiful harps thro' all the choir.
 Beautiful strains, etc.

Beautiful crowns on every brow,
Beautiful palms the conquerors show,
Beautiful robes the ransomed wear,
Beautiful all who enter there.
 Beautiful robes, etc.,

Beautiful throne of Christ our King,
Beautiful songs the angels sing;
Beautiful rest, all wanderings cease,
Beautiful home of perfect peace.
 Beautiful rest, etc.

IF I WERE A SUNBEAM.

[From the Golden Shower, page 40.]

If I were a sunbeam, I know what I'd do,
I would seek white lilies, roaming woodlands thro',
I would steal among them, softest light I'd shed;
Until every lily raised its drooping head,
 Until every lilly raised its drooping head.

If I were a sunbeam, I know where I'd go;
Into lowliest hovels, dark with want and woe
Till sad hearts look'd upward, I would shine and shine!
Then they'd think of heaven, their sweet home and mine,
 Then they'd think of heaven, their sweet home and mine.

Art thou not a sunbeam, child, whose life is glad
With an inner radiance sunshine never had?
Oh, as God hath blessed thee, scatter rays divine!
For there is no sunbeam but must die or shine.
 For their is no sumbeam but must die or shine.

MAN THE LIFE-BOAT!

[Fron the Golden Censer, page 57.]

Man the life-boat! man the life-boat!
　　Hearts of love, your succor lend!
See the shattered vessel staggers!
　　Quick! O quick! assistance lend!
Now the fragile boat is hanging
　　On the billow's feathery height;
Now 'midst fearful depths descending,
　　While we wither at the sight.

Courage! courage! she's in safety!
　　See again her buoyant form,
By his gracious hand uplifted,
　　Who controls the raging storm.
With her precious cargo freighted,
　　Now the life-boat nears the shore;
Parents, brethren, friends, embracing,
　　Those they thought to see no more.

Christian, pause, and deeply ponder;
　　Is there nothing you can do?
The sinking ship, the storm, the life-boat,
　　Have they not a voice for you?
There's a storm, a fearful tempest—
　　Souls are sinking in despair;
There's a shore of blessed refuge,
　　Try, O try to guide them there.

O, remember Him who saved you,
　　Whose right hand deliverance wrought,
Who, from depths of guilt and anguish,
　　You to peace and safety brought;
'Tis His voice who cheers you onward—
　　"He that winneth souls is wise;"
Launch the Gospel's blessed life-boat;
　　Venture all to win the prize.

SWEET HOUR OF PRAYER.

[From the Golden Chain, page 10.]

Sweet hour of prayer! sweet hour of prayer!
That calls me from a world of care,
And bids me at my Father's throne
Make all my wants and wishes known:
In seasons of distress and grief,
My soul has often found relief;
And oft escaped the tempter's snare
By thy return, sweet hour of prayer,
And oft escaped the tempter's snare
By thy return, sweet hour of prayer.

Sweet hour of prayer! sweet hour of prayer!
Thy wings shall my petition bear,
To him whose truth and faithfulness,
Engage the waiting soul to bless;
And since he bids me seek his face,
Believe his word, and trust his grace,
I'll cast on him my every care,
And wait for thee, sweet hour of prayer!

Sweet hour of prayer! sweet hour of prayer!
May I thy consolation share;
Till, from Mount Pisgah's lofty height,
I view my home, and take my flight:
This robe of flesh I'll drop, and rise
To seize the everlasting prize.

JESUS LOVES ME.

[From the Golden Shower, page 68.]

Jesus loves me! this I know,
For the Bible tells me so,
Little ones to him belong,
They are weak but He is strong.
Yes, Jesus loves me,
Yes, Jesus loves me,
Yes, Jesus loves me,
The Bible tells me so.

Jesus loves me! He who died,
Heaven's gate to open wide;
He will wash away my sin,
Let his little child come in.
 Yes, Jesus loves me, etc.

Jesus loves me! loves me still,
Though I'm very weak and ill;
From his shining throne on high,
Comes to watch me where I lie.
 Yes, Jesus loves me, etc.

Jesus loves me! He will stay
Close beside me, all the way
If I love him, when I die
He will take me home on high.
 Yes, Jesus loves me, etc.

PEACEFULLY SLEEP.

[From the Golden Chain, page 24.]
Peacefully lay her down to rest,
Place the turf kindly on her breast;
Sweet is the slumber beneath the sod,
While the pure soul is resting with God.
 Peacefully sleep, peacefully sleep,
 Sleep till that morning, peacefully sleep.

Close to herlone and narrow house,
Gracefully ave, ye willow boughs;
Flowers of the wildwood, your odors shed
Over the holy beautiful dead.
 Peacefully sleep, etc.

Quietly sleep, beloved one,
Rest from thy toil—thy labor is done;
Rest till the trump from the opening skies
Bid thee from dust to glory arise!
 Peacefully sleep, etc.

WHO SHALL SING?

[From the Golden Chain, page 14.]

Who shall sing if not the children,
  Did not Jesus die for them?
May they not, with other jewels,
  Sparkle in his diadem?
Why unless the song of heaven
  They begin to practice here?
Why to them were voices given,
  Bird-like voices, sweet and clear?

There's a choir of infant songsters,
  White-robed, round the Saviour's throne;
Angels cease, and, waiting, listen!
  Oh! 'tis sweeter than their own!
Faith can hear the rapturous choral,
  When her ear is upward turned;
Is not this the same, perfected,
  Which upon the earth they learned?

Jesus, when on earth sojourning,
  Loved them with a wondrous love;
And will he, to heaven returning,
  Faithless to his blessing prove?
Oh! they can not sing too early!
  Fathers, stand not in their way!
Birds do sing while day is breaking—
  Tell me, then, why should not they?

JUST AS I AM.

[Tune, *Woodworth.*]

Just as I am, without one plea,
But that thy blood was shed for me,
And that thou bidd'st me come to thee,
  O Lamb of God, I come!

Just as I am, and waiting not
To rid my soul of one dark blot,
To thee, whose blood can cleanse each spot,
    O Lamb of God, I come!

Just as I am, though tossed about
With many a conflict, many a doubt,
Fighting within, and fears without,
    O Lamb of God, I come!

Just as I am, poor, wretched, blind—
Sight, riches, healing of the mind,
Yea, all I need, in thee to find,
    O Lamb of God I come!

Just as I am, thou wilt receive,
Wilt welcome, pardon, cleanse, relieve,
Because thy promise, I believe,
    O Lamb of God, I come!

Just as I am, thy love, unknown,
Has broken every barrier down;
Now to be thine, yea, thine alone,
    O Lamb of God, I come!

JOY FOR THE SORROWFUL.

[From the Golden Shower, page 110.]

Joy for the sorrowful, strength for the weak,
Words of benevolence Jesus doth speak;
His purpose of mercy no power can stay,
For sorrow and sighing shall both flee away,
For sorrow and sighing shall both flee away.
    His purpose of mercy no power can stay,
    For sorrow and sighing shall both flee away,
    For sorrow and sighing shall both flee away.

Joy for the sorrowful, sight for the blind,
The dumb singing praises, the savage made kind,

.The lame leaping high; these are signs of the day,
When sorrow and sighing shall both flee away.
  The lame leaping high, these are the signs of the day,etc.

Joy for the sorrowful, laughter and song,
Among the redeemed, who journey along,
All looking for rest at the end of the way,
When sorrow and sighing shall both flee away,
  All looking for rest, at the end of the way, etc.

Joy for the sorrowful! Spirit of God,
If on toward Zion but feebly I've trod,
O, strengthen my soul, and still lead me I pray,
Till sorrow and sighing have both fled away.
  O, strengthen my soul, and still lead me I pray, etc.

FAR OUT UPON THE PRAIRIE.

[From the Golden Chain, page 20.]

Far out upon the prairie
  How many children dwell,
Who never read the Bible,
  Or hear the Sabbath bell;
And when the holy morning
  Wakes us to sing and pray,
They spend the precious moments
  In idleness and play.
    Far out upon the prairie
      How many children dwell,
    Who never read the Bible,
      Or hear the Sabbath bell.

For they have no kind pastor,
  Whose loving words have told
Of Jesus, the good Shepherd,
  And called them to his fold;
No Sabbath-school inviting
  Its pleasant doors within,
No teacher's voice entreating
  To leave the way of sin.
    Far out, etc.

I wish that I could tell them
  How Jesus came to die,
When he for little children
  Left his bright throne on high;
And all the sad, sad story
  Of sorrow which he bore,
When for his crown of glory
  A crown of thorns he wore.
    Far out, etc.

And so each morn and evening,
  Whene'er I kneel in prayer,
I'll ask the gracious Saviour
  To send his gospel there;
That in the glorious city
  In which he dwells above,
We all may sing together
  Of his redeeming love.
    Far out, etc.

THE LAND OF BEULAH. C. M.

[From the Golden Shower, page 50.]

My latest sun is sinking fast,
  My race is nearly run,
My strongest trials now are past,
  My triumph is begun.
    O come, angel band, come and around me stand,
    O bear me away on your snowy wings,
    To my immortal home,
    O bear me away on your snowy wings,
    To my immortal home.

I know I'm nearing the holy ranks,
  Of friends and kindred dear,
For I brush the dews on Jordan's banks,
  The crossing must be near.
    O come, angel band, etc.

I've almost gained my heavenly home,
  My spirit loudly sings;
The holy ones, behold they come!
  I hear the noise of wings.
      O come, angel band, etc.

O, bear my longing heart to him
  Who bled and died for me;
Whose blood now cleanses from all sin,
  And gives me victory.
      O come, angel band, etc.,

COME UNTO ME.   Chant.

[From the Golden Shower, page 101.]

With tearful eyes I look around,
  Life seems a dark and stormy sea;
Yet, 'midst the gloom I hear a sound,
  A heavenly whisper, Come to me.

It tells me of a place of rest—
  It tells me where my soul may flee:
Oh! to the weary, faint, opprest,
  How sweet the bidding, Come to me.

When nature shudders, loth to part
  From all I love, enjoy and see;
When a faint chill steals o'er my heart,
  A sweet voice utters, Come to me.

Come, for all else must fall and die,
  Earth is no resting place for thee:
Heavenward direct thy weeping eye,
  I am thy portion, Come to me.

O voice of mercy! voice of love!
  In conflict, grief, and agony,
Support me, cheer me from above!
  And gently whisper, Come to me.

4

POOR PILGRIM.

[From the Golden Censer, page 78.]

Come, poor pilgrim, sad and weary,
  Why heaves thy breast?
Roaming this wide world so dreary,
  Sighing for rest.
There is rest for thee in glory,
  Among the blest;
Listen to the joyful story,
  There, there is rest.
      There is rest, sweet rest,
      There is rest, sweet rest,
     Where the wicked cease from troubling,
      And the weary are at rest,
     Where the wicked cease from troubling,
      And the weary are at rest.

There are those who've gone before us,
  All who are blest;
Singing now the happy chorus,
  There, there is rest.
There the golden harps are ringing,
  Harps of the blest;
And the angel bands are singing,
  There, there is rest.
      There, there is rest, etc.

And, while we on earth are praying,
  Jesus the blest
Unto us is sweetly saying,
  There, there is rest.
We shall meet where parting never,
  Comes to the blest;
And we'll safely dwell forever
  In heavenly rest.
      There, there is rest, etc.

WE ARE COMING, BLESSED SAVIOUR.

[From the Golden Censer, page 17.]

We are coming, blessed Saviour,
  We hear thy gentle voice;
We would be thine forever,
  And in thy love rejoice.
     We are coming, we are coming,
      We are coming, blessed Saviour,
     We are coming, we are coming,
      We hear thy gentle voice.

We are coming, blessed Saviour,
  To meet that happy band,
And sing with them forever,
  And in thy presence stand.
     We are coming, etc.,
      To meet that happy band.

We are coming, blessed Saviour,
  Our Father's house we see—
A glorious mansion ever
  For children young as we.
     We are coming, etc.,
      Our Father's house we see.

We are coming, blessed Saviour,
  That happy home is ours;
If here we gain thy favor,
  We'll reach those fragrant bowers.
     We are coming, etc.,
      That happy home is ours.

We are coming, blessed Saviour,
  To crown our Jesus King,
And then with angels ever
  His praises we will sing.
     We are coming, etc.,
      To crown our Jesus King.

GOING HOME.

[From the Golden, Shower, page 64.]

Through a strange country as pilgrims we stray,
  For we're going, going, going home,
Onward we go through the swift fading day,
  For we're going, going, going home.
Weary our march since the fair rosy dawn,
Long is the distance we've traveled since morn,
But we regret not the hours that are gone,
  For we're going, going, going home.

Why should we gather earth's withering flowers,
  When we're going. going, going home.
Soon shall we tread the fair Heavenly bowers,
  For we're going, going, going home;
There, fragrant garlands immortal will bloom,
Untouched by blight, and unshadowed by gloom,
And never strewing the path to the tomb;
  For we're going, going, going home..

Hark! 'tis the storm crashing loud through the pines,
  We are going, going, going home;
See the faint glimmering light that now shines,
  We are going, going, going home.
Little we heed the wild roar of the wind,
Onward we still look, and never behind:
This thought alone gives sweet peace to our mind,
  We're going, going, going home.

Soon we shall hear the glad welcoming voice,
  We're going, going, going home:
Bidding our spirits forever rejoice,
  We are going, going, going home:
Home to our mansion prepared in the sky,
Where we can never more suffer or die.
O! let our anthem of praise ring on high,
  We are going, going, going home.

BLESSED BIBLE.

[From the Golden Censer, page 42.]

Blessed Bible! how I love it!
  How it doth my bosom cheer!
What on earth like this to covet?
  Oh, what stores of wealth are here!
Man was lost and doom'd to sorrow,
  Not one ray of light or bliss
Could he from earth's treasures borrow,
  Till his way was cheered by this.
      Blessed Bible, blessed Bible,
      How thou dost my spirit cheer.

Yes, I'll to my bosom press thee;
  Precious Word, I'll hide thee here,
Sure my very heart will bless thee,
  For thou ever say'st "Good cheer!"
Speak, poor heart, and tell thy pond'rings,
  Tell how far thy rovings led,
When this book brought back thy wand'rings,
  Speaking life as from the dead.
      Blessed Bible, etc.

Yes, sweet Bible! I will hide thee
  Deep—yes, deeper in this heart;
Thou through all my life wilt guide me,
  And in death we will not part.
Part in death? no, never! never!
  Through death's vale I'll lean on thee;
Then in worlds above, forever
  Sweeter till thy truths shall be.
      Blessed Bible, etc.

GOOD TIDINGS.

[From the Golden Shower, page 36.]

Shout the tidings of salvation,
  To the aged and the young;
Till the precious invitation
  Waken every heart and tongue.

Send the sound the earth around,
From the rising to the setting of the sun,
Till each gath'ring crowd shall proclaim aloud
The glorious work is done.

Shout the tidings of salvation,
O'er the prairies of the West;
Till each gath'ring congregation
With the gospel sound in blest.
Send the sound, etc.

Shout the tidings of salvation,
Mingling with the ocean's roar,
Till the ships of every nation,
Bear the news from shore to shore.
Send the sound, etc.

Shout the tidings of salvation
O'er the islands of the sea;
Till in humble adoration,
All to Christ shall bow the knee.
Send the sound, etc.

SCATTER SMILES AS YOU GO.

[From the Golden Censer, page 82.]

Scatter smiles, bright smiles, as you pass on your way,
Thro' this world of toil and care;
Like the beams of the morning that gently play,
They will leave a sunlight there.
Scatter smiles, bright smiles,
Scatter smiles as you pass on your way,
Scatter smiles, bright smiles,
Scatter smiles, bright smiles.

Scattter smiles, bright smiles, 'tis but little they cost;
But your heart may never know
What a joy they may carry to weary ones
Who are pale with want and woe.
Scatter smiles, bright smiles, etc.

Scatter smiles, bright smiles, o'er the grave of the past,
   Where the orphan's treasure lies;
In the tear-drop that glistens there light will shine,
   As the rainbow paints the skies.
      Scatter smiles, bright smiles, etc.

Scatter smiles, bright smiles, o'er the young who have strayed,
   From the path where once they trod;
You may lead to the fountain of truth again,
   You may bring them home to God.
      Scatter smiles, bright smiles, etc.

Scatter smiles, bright smiles, as you pass on your way
   Through this world of toil and care;
Like the beams of the morning that gently play,
   They will leave a sunlight there.
      Scatter smiles, bright smiles, etc.

SWEET REST IN HEAVEN.

[From the Golden Shower, page 103.]

Come schoolmates, don't grow weary,
   But let us journey on,
The moments will not tarry,
   This life will soon be gone.
      There is sweet rest in heaven,
      There is sweet rest in heaven,
      There is sweet rest, there is sweet rest,
      There is sweet rest in heaven.

We've listed for the army,
   We've listed for the war,
We'll fight until we conquer,
   By faith and humble prayer.
      There is sweet rest, etc.

Our Captain's gone before us,
   He bids us all to come;
High up in endless glory,
   He's fitted up our home.
      There is sweet rest, etc.,

And Jesus will be with us, .
   E'en to our journey's end;
In every sore affliction
   His "present help" to lend.
      There is sweet rest, etc.

Then glory be to Jesus,
   Who bought us with his blood;
And glory be to Jesus,
   Who gives us every good.
      There is sweet rest, etc.

"YOUR SAVIOUR WEPT."

[From the Golden Censer, page 26.]

How sweet in every trying scene,
   That wounds the spirit here,
To feel that Jesus bore our grief,
   And know he still is near;
O ye who o'er the couch of death
   Your lonely watch have kept,
Tho' anguish rend your aching breast,
   Remember Jesus wept.

He groaned in spirit while he spoke;
   "Where have you laid the dead?"
"Lord, come and see," they murmured low,
   He followed where they led;
Beneath a cold sepulchral stone
   An only brother slept,
And angels wondered as they gazed,
   For lo! the Saviour wept.

How oft the prayer our lips would breathe,
   The heart alone may speak;
How oft the penitential tear
   Bedews the mourner's cheek;
Poor child of toil, though dark and sad,
   Thy weary lot may be,
With few to smooth life's rugged path,
   Thy Saviour wept for thee.

"WE'LL ALL MEET AGAIN IN THE MORNING."

[From the Golden Shower, page 106.]

A little child lay dying
  As the sunset hour drew nigh,
And these the words he uttered
  When he breathed his last Good-bye,
"I know that my angel mother
  Is waiting to bear me from thee,
We'll all meet again in the morning,
  Dear father weep not for me!"
      We'll all meet again in the morning,
      We'll all meet again in the morning
      We'll all meet again in the morning,
      Of heaven's eternal day.

The words were full of solace,
  Falling like a healing balm
On the heart so sorely stricken,
  That the mourner might well be calm.
The sharp sting of anguish taken,
  The burden of grief grew more light,
We'll all meet again in the morning,
  Like a rainbow spanned Death's night.
      We'll all meet, etc.

O, ye who sadly languish,
  Weighed down by grief and gloom,
Beside the grave's dark portal,
  Look beyond the silent tomb!
With God leave your precious treasures,
  Shall he not in all things do right?
We'll all meet again in the morning
  Death's sleep is but for a night.
      We'll all meet, etc.

- COME TO JESUS.

[From the Happy Voices, page 40.]

Come to Jesus, Come to Jesus,
  Come to Jesus to-day;
To-day come to Jesus,
  Come to Jesus to-day;

He will save you, he will save you.
  He will save you to-day;
To-day he will save you,
  He will save you to-day.

Don't reject him, don't reject him,
  Don't reject him to-day,
To-day don't reject him,
  Don't reject him to-day.

He is ready, he is ready,
  He is ready to-day;
To-day he is ready,
  He is ready to-day.

Oh believe him, oh believe him,
  Oh believe him to-day;
To-day oh believe him,
  Oh believe him to-day.

Do not tarry, do not tarry,
  Do not tarry to-day,
To-day do not tarry,
  Do not tarry to-day.

Hallelujah, Hallelujah,
  Hallelujah, Amen;
Amen, Hallelujah,
  Hallelujah, Amen.

ALWAYS SPEAK THE TRUTH.

[From the Happy Voices, page 77.]

Be the matter what it may,
  Always speak the truth :
Whether work or whether play,
  Always speak the truth.
Never from this rule depart,
Grave it deeply on your heart,
Written 'tis in virtue's chart ;
  Always speak the truth.

There's a charm in verity—
  Always speak the truth ;
But there's meanness in a lie—
  Always speak the truth.
He is but a coward slave
Who, a present pain to waive,
Stoops to falsehood; then be brave
  Always speak the truth.

Falsehood seldom stands alone—
  Always speak the truth ;
One begets another one—
  Always speak the truth.
Falsehood all the soul degrades,
'Tis a sin from which proceeds
Greater sins and darker deeds ;
  Always speak the truth.

When you're wrong the folly own ;
  Always speak the truth ;
Here's a victory to be won,
  Always speak the truth.
He who speaks with lying tongue
Adds to wrong a greater wrong ;
Then with courage true and strong
  Always speak the truth.

SINNERS ENTREATED.

[From the Happy Voices, page 66.]

Sinners will you scorn the message
  Sent in mercy from above ?
Every sentence, oh how tender!
  Every line is full of love ;
     Listen to it ;
  Every line is full of love.

Hear the heralds of the gospel
  News from Zion's king proclaim,
To each rebel sinner, "Pardon,
  Free forgiveness in his name,"
     How important!
  Free forgiveness in his name.

Oh ye angels hovering round us,
  Waiting spirits, speed your way,
Hasten to the court of heaven,
  Tidings bear without delay ;
     Rebel sinners
  Glad the message will obey.

THE LAND BEYOND THE RIVER.

[From the Golden Censer, page 35.]

No mortal eye that land hath seen,
  Beyond, beyond the river,
Its smiling valleys, hills so green,
  Beyond, beyond the river.
Its shores are coming nearer,
The skies are growing clearer,
Each day it seemeth dearer,
  That land beyond the river.
    We'll stand the storm, we'll stand the storm,
    Its rage is almost over,
    We'll anchor in the harbor soon,
    In the land beyond the river.

No cankering care nor mortal strife,
  Beyond, beyond the river,
But happy, never ending life,
  Beyond, beyond the river.
Thro' the eternal hours,
  God's love, in heavenly showers,
Shall water faith's fair flowers
  In the land beyond the river.
      We'll stand the storm, etc.

That glorious day will ne'er be done,
  Beyond, beyond the river.
When we've the crown and kingdom won,
  Beyond, beyond the river.
There is eternal pleasure,
And joys that none can measure,
For those who have their treasure,
  In the land beyond the river.
      We'll stand the storm, etc.

When shall we look from Zion's hill,
  Beyond, beyond the river,
With endless bliss our hearts shall thrill,
  Beyond, beyond the river.
There angels bright are singing,
Where golden harps are ringing,
We ne'er shall cease our singing,
  In the land beyond the river.
      We'll stand the storm, etc.

PORTUGUESE HYMN.

[From the Happy Voices, page 49.]

How firm a foundation, ye saints of the Lord,
Is laid for your faith in his excellent word,
What more can he say than to you he hath **said**,
Who unto the Saviour for refuge have **fled**,
Who unto the Saviour for refuge have **fled**.

Fear not, I am with thee: Oh be not dismayed,
For I am thy God, and will still give thee aid;
I'll strengthen thee, help thee, and cause thee to stand
Upheld by my righteous, omnipotent hand.   .

When through the deep waters I call thee to go,
The rivers of sorrow shall not overflow;
For I will be with thee thy trials to bless,
And sanctify to thee thy deepest distress.

The soul that on Jesus hath leaned for repose,
I will not, I will not desert to his foes;
That soul, though all hell should endeavor to shake,
I'll never—no, never—no, never forsake.

THE CHILD'S DESIRE.

[From the Happy Voices, page 27.]

I think when I read that sweet story of old,
    When Jesus was here among men,
How he called little children as lambs to his fold,
    I should like to have been with them then.

I wish that his hands had been placed on my head,
    That his arm had been thrown around me,
And that I might have seen his kind look when he said
    " Let the little ones come unto me."

Yet still to his footstool in prayer I may go,
    And ask for a share in his love;
And if I thus earnestly seek him below,
    I shall see him and hear him above.

In that beautiful place he has gone to prepare
    For all who are washed and forgiven;
And many dear children are gathering there,
    " For of such is the kingdom of heaven."

"NEVER BE AFRAID."

[From the Golden Censer, page 20.]

Never be afraid to speak for Jesus,
  Think how much a word can do;
Never be afraid to own your Saviour,
  He who loves and cares for you.
        Never be afraid, never be afraid,
          Never, never, never,
        Jesus is your loving Saviour,
          Therefore never be afraid.

Never be afraid to work for Jesus,
  In his vineyard day by day;
Labor with a kind and willing spirit,
  He will all your toil repay.
        Never be afraid, etc.

Never be afraid to bear for Jesus,
  Keen reproaches when they fall;
Patiently endure your every trial,
  Jesus meekly bore them all.
        Never be afraid, etc.

Never be afraid to live for Jesus,
  If you on his care depend,
Safely shall you pass through every trial,
  He will bring you to the end.
        Never be afraid, etc.

Never be afraid to die for Jesus;
  He the life, the truth, the way,
Gently in his arms of love will bear you
  To the realms of endless day.
        Never be afraid, etc.

WHO IS MY NEIGHBOR?

[From the Golden Censer, page 24.]

O, who is my neighbor? pray tell me,
　As I journey along here below;
For my Bible commands me to love him
　As myself, and my neighbor I'd know;
Is it he who sits down at my table,
　My brother so dear unto me,
Or my friend who hath done me a favor,—
　My neighbor, O where may he be?
　　　　Where may he be? where may he be?
　　　　My neighbor, oh! where may he be?

The world is thy neighbor, poor pilgrim;
　From the beggar so wretched to see,
To the rich man that rides in his carriage,—
　All alike have a claim upon thee!
Go ye out in the highways and hedges,
　The alleys, the lanes. and the street;
For ye never have need to stand idle
　The want of a neighbor to greet!
　　　　A neighbor to greet,—a neighbor to greet!
　　　　The want of a neighbor to greet.

Drink deep from sweet charity's fountain;
　Little failings in kindness o'erlook;
For our Saviour had pity for others,
　And he never his neighbor forsook.
　　　　He never forsook, etc.

He hath said that a cup of cold water,
　If given in the name of the Lord,
In that day when he makes up his jewels,
　Shall meet with a tenfold reward!
　　　　A tenfold reward, etc.

WEBB.

[From the Golden Chain, page 104.]

The morning light is breaking,
  The darkness disappears;
The sons of earth are waking
  To penitential tears:
Each breeze that sweeps the ocean
  Brings tidings from afar
Of nations in commotion
  Prepared for Zion's war.

Rich dews of grace come o'er us,
  In many a gentle shower,
And brighter scenes before us
  Are opening every hour:
Each cry to heaven going
  Abundant answer brings,
And heavenly gales are blowing
  With peace upon their wings.

See heathen nations bending
  Before the God of love,
And thousand hearts ascending
  In gratitude above:
While sinners, now confessing,
  The gospel's call obey,
And seek a Saviour's blessing,
  A nation in a day.

Blest river of salvation,
  Pursue thy onward way;
Flow thou to every nation,
  Nor in thy richness stay:
Stay not till all the lowly
  Triumphant reach their home,
Stay not till all the holy
  Proclaim the Lord is come.

5

WE'LL STAND FOR THE RIGHT, OR LIFE'S BATTLE.

[From the Golden Chain, page 82.]

This life is a battle with Satan and sin,
And we are the soldiers the victory to win;
And Christ is the Captain of our little band,
Whatever opposes, for him we shall stand.
 We will stand for the right,
 We will stand for the right,
 We will stand, we will stand for the right.

To God, for our armor, we'll fail not to go,
He'll clothe us with truth and with righteousness too:
The "Gospel of peace" shall our footsteps attend,
The "good shield of faith" from all harm shall defend.
 We will stand, etc.

Salvation our helmet, the Bible our sword,
Tho' wily our foes, we're "strong in the Lord;"
While watching and praying our armor keeps bright,
Our Jesus will help us to stand for the right.
 We will stand, etc.

Tho' little temptations (the worst ones of all)
Will often beset us, to make us to fall;
We'll "stand up for Jesus," and, when life is o'er,
For us He'll be standing on Jordan's bright shore.
 We will stand, etc.

THE SHINING SHORE.

[From the Golden Chain, page 83.]

My days are gliding swiftly by,
 And I, a pilgrim stranger,
Would not detain them as they fly!
 Those hours of toil and danger,
  For oh! we stand on Jordan's strand,
  Our friends are passing over,
  And just before, the shining shore
  We may almost discover.

We'll gird our loins, my brethren dear,
  Our distant home discerning;
Our absent Lord has left us word,
  Let every lamp be burning—
    For oh! etc.

Should coming days be cold and dark,
  We need not cease our singing;
That perfect rest naught can molest,
  Where golden harps are ringing.
    For oh! etc.

Let sorrow's rudest tempest blow,
  Each chord on earth to sever,
Our King says, come, and there's our home,
  Forever, oh! forever!
    For oh! etc.

"TO-DAY."

[From the Happy Voices, page 79.]

To-day the Saviour calls;
  Ye wand'rers come;
Oh, ye benighted souls,
  Why longer roam?

To-day the Saviour calls,
  For refuge fly;
The storm of vengeance falls,
  Ruin is nigh.

To-day the Saviour calls,
  Oh listen now;
Within these sacred walls,
  To Jesus bow.

The Spirit calls to-day,
  Yield to his power;
Oh grieve him not away,
  'Tis mercy's hour.

FRIEND EVER NEAR.

[From the Happy Voices, page 66.]

One there is above all others .
  Well deserves the name of friend;
His is love beyond a brother's,
  Costly, free, and knows no end.
Which of all our friends, to save us,
  Could or would have shed his blood?
But our Jesus died to have us
  Reconciled in him to God.

When he lived on earth abased,
  "Friend of sinners" was his name;
Now above all glory raised,
  He rejoices in the same. . . .
Oh for grace our hearts to soften!
  Teach us, Lord, at length to love
We, alas, forget too often, .
  What a friend we have above.

EXPOSTULATION.

[From the Happy Voices, page 78.]

Oh turn ye, oh turn ye, for why will ye die?
Since God in great mercy is coming so nigh,
Since Jesus invites you, the spirit says come,
And angels are waiting to welcome you home.

How vain the delusion that, while you delay,
Your hearts may grow better, your chains melt away;
Come wretched, come guilty, come just as you are,
All helpless and dying, to Jesus repair.

The contrite in heart he will freely receive,
Oh why will you not the glad message believe?
If sin be your burden, oh, will you not come?
'Tis he makes you welcome, he bids you come home.

A CHRISTMAS CAROL.

[From the Golden Chain, page 86.]

Joy to the sons of men
　On this bright Christmas morn!
List to the welcome words again
　That charm our waiting hearts, as when
The shepherds heard with glad amaze
　Th' announcement of angelic lays,
　　" A Saviour Christ is born,
　　A Saviour Christ is born,
　　A Saviour Christ is born."

Joy to earth's sorrowing child,
　On this calm peaceful morn!
The holy, harmless, undefiled,
　Can soothe his breast with comfort mild;
The hymn that floats along the air,
　Shall find an answer echoing there—
　　The Saviour, etc.

Joy to the sick and poor,
　"Blessed are they that mourn;"
If they submissively endure,
　And trust his holy promise sure:
He comes all sorrow to relieve,
　To comfort all who will believe—
　　The Saviour, etc.

Love, joy, good-will, and peace,
　Since that first Christmas morn,
Have come to earth, and ne'er shall cease,
　To Him who purchased our release,
Our hearts, redeemed from death, we'll bring,
　And humbly, gratefully we'll sing.
　　The Saviour, etc.

SING HIS PRAISE.

[From the Happy Voices, page 77.]

Would you be as angels are ?
  Sing, oh sing his praise ;
Would you banish every care ?
  Sing, oh sing his praise
Like the lark upon the wing,
Like the warbling bird of spring,
Like the crystal spheres that ring,
  Sing, oh sing his praise.

If the world upon you frown,
  Sing, oh sing his praise,
If your'e left to sing alone,
  Sing, oh sing his praise ;
If sad trials come to you,
As to every one they do,
For that they are blessings too,
  Sing, oh sing his praise,

OLIVET.

[From the Happy Voices, page 41.]

My faith looks up to thee,
Thou Lamb of Calvary,
  Saviour divine ;
Now hear me while I pray,
Take all my guilt away,
Oh let me from this day
  Be wholly thine.

May thy rich grace impart
Strength to my fainting heart,
  My zeal inspire :
As though hast died for me,
Oh may my love to thee
Pure, warm, and changeless be,
  A living fire.

While life's dark maze I tread,
And griefs around me spread,
    Be thou my guide ;
Bid darkness turn to day,
Wipe sorrow's tears away,
Nor let me ever stray
    From thee aside.

When ends life's transient dream,
When death's cold, sullen stream
    Shall o'er me roll,
Blest Saviour, then in love
Fear and distrust remove ;
Oh bear me safe above,
    A ransomed soul.

THE YOUNG DISCIPLE.

[From the Happy Voices, page 43.]

Oh happy day that fixed my choice
    On thee, my Saviour and my God ,
Well may this glowing heart rejoice,
    And tell its raptures all abroad.
        Happy day, happy day ! etc.

'Tis done, the great transaction's done :
    I am my Lord's and he is mine ;
He drew me, and I followed on,
    Charmed to confess the voice divine,
        Happy day, happy day ! etc.

High heaven that heard the solemn vow,
    That vow renewed shall daily hear,
Till in life's latest hour I bow,
    And bless in death a bond so dear.
        Happy day, happy day ! etc.

O, WE ARE VOLUNTEERS.

[From the Golden Censer, page 88.]

O. we are volunteers in the army of the Lord,
Forming into line at our Captain's word;
We are under marching orders to take the battle-field,
And we'll ne'er give o'er the fight till the foe shall yield.

> Come and join the army, the army of the Lord,
> Jesus is our Captain, we rally at his word;
> Sharp will be the conflict with the pow'rs of sin,
> But with such a Leader, we are sure to win.

The glory of our flag is the emblem of the dove,
Gleaming are our swords from the forge of love;
We go forth, but not to battle for earthly honors vain,
'Tis a bright immortal crown that we seek to gain.

> Come and join the army, etc.

Our foes are in the field, pressing hard on ev'ry side,—
Envy, anger, hatred, with self and pride;
They are cruel, fierce and strong, ever ready to attack,
We must watch, and fight, and pray, if we'd drive them
   back.

> Come and join the army, etc.

O. glorious is the struggle in which we draw the sword,
Glorious is the Kingdom of Christ, our Lord;
It shall spread from sea to sea, it shall reach from shore to
   shore,
And His people shall be blessed for evermore.

> Come and join the army, etc.

FOUNT.

[From the Happy Voices, page 66.]

Come thou fount of every blessing,
   Tune my heart to sing thy grace;
Streams of mercy never ceasing,
   Call for songs of loudest praise;
Teach me some melodious sonnet,
   Sung by flaming tongues above;
Praise the mount—I'm fixed upon it—
   Mount of God's unchanging love.

Here I raise my Ebenezer,
   Hither by thy help I'm come,
And I hope, by thy good pleasure,
   Safely to arrive at home.
Jesus sought me when a stranger,
   Wandering from the fold of God;
He to rescue me from danger,
   Interposed his precious blood.

Oh to grace how great a debtor
   Daily I'm constrained to be!
Let that grace now like a fetter,
   Bind my wandering soul to thee;
Prone to wander, Lord I feel it—
   Prone to leave the God I love;
Here's my heart—oh take and seal it,
   Seal it from thy courts above.

THE PASTURE.

[From the Happy Voices, page 84.]

Faithful Shepherd, meek and mild,
To thy pastures lead a child,
Where the tender verdure grows,
Where the peaceful streamlet flows,
Where thy flock from danger free,
Hear thy voice and follow thee.

There beneath thy watchful eye,
They are safe, though danger's nigh;
There enfolded in thy arms,
They can smile at rude alarms;
Though a host their way oppose,
Thou wilt save them from their foes.

When the vale of grief they tread,
Thou dost mark the tears they shed;
By their side in pity stand,
Dry the tear with tender hand;
Gently quell the rising fear,
Make it sweet to suffer there.

Faithful Shepherd, meek and mild,
To thy pastures lead a child;
Weak and helpless Lord, I am,
Gather in a wandering lamb;
Lest from thee I further stray,
Take me to thy fold I pray.

HAPPY DAY.

[From the Happy Voices, page 43.]
Preserved by thine almighty power,
  Oh Lord, our Maker, Saviour, King,
And bro't to see this happy hour,
  We come thy praises here to sing.
    Happy day, happy day,
    Here in thy courts we'll gladly stay,
    And at thy footstool humbly pray
    That thou wouldst take our sins away;
    Happy day, happy day,
    When Christ shall wash our sins away.

We praise thee for thy constant care,
  For life preserved, for mercies given;
Oh may we still those mercies share,
  And taste the joys of sin forgiven.
    Happy day, happy day, etc.

And when on earth our days are done,
   Grant, Lord, that we at length may join,
Teachers and scholars round thy throne,
   The song of Moses and the Lamb.
     Happy day, happy day, etc.

THAT BEAUTIFUL LAND.

[From the Golden Censer, page 66.]

A beautiful land by faith I see,
A land of rest, from sorrow free;
The home of the ramsoned, bright and fair,
And beautiful angels too are there.
     Will you go? will you go?
     Go to that beautiful land with me?
     Will you go? will you go?
     Go to that beautiful land?

That beautiful land, the City of Light,
It ne'er has known the shades of night;
The glory of God, the light of day
Hath driven the darkness far away.
     Will you go, etc.

In vision I see its streets of gold,
Its beautiful gates I too behold,
The river of life, the crystal sea,
The ambrosial fruit of life's fair tree.
     Will you go, etc.

The heavenly throng arrayed in white,
In rapture range the plains of light;
And in one harmonious choir they praise
Their glorious Saviour's matchless grace.
     Will you go, etc.

OUR BRIGHT HOME ABOVE.

[From the Golden Censer, page 71.]

We are going, we are going,
  To a home beyond the skies,
Where the fields are robed in beauty,
  And the sunlight never dies.
Where the fount of joy is flowing
  In the valley green and fair,
We shall dwell in love together,
  There will be no parting there.
      We are going, we are going,
        To a home beyond the skies,
      Where the fields are robed in beauty,
        And the sunlight never dies.

We are going, we are going,
  And the music we have heard
Like the echo of the woodland,
  Or the carol of a bird;
With the rosy light of morning
  On the calm and fragrant air,
Still it murmurs, softly murmurs,
  There will be no parting there.
      We are going, etc.

We are going, we are going,
  Where the day of life is o'er
To that pure and happy region
  Where our friends have gone before;
They are singing with the angels
  In that land so bright and fair;
We shall dwell with them forever,
  There will be no parting there.
      We are going, etc.

THE GOLDEN SHORE; OR A HOME BEYOND THE TIDE.

[From the Golden Chain, page 87.]

GIRLS. We are out on the ocean sailing,
 Homeward bound we sweetly glide:
BOYS. We are out on the ocean sailing,
 To a home beyond the tide.
GIRLS. Millions now are safely landed,
 Over on the golden shore:
BOYS. Millions more are on their journey,
 Yet there's room for millions more.
CHORUS.—All the storms will soon be over,
 Then we'll anchor in the harbor:
We are out on the ocean sailing,
 To a home beyond the tide;
We are out on the ocean sailing,
 To a home beyond the tide.

GIRLS. Spread your sails, while heavenly breezes
 Gently waft our vessel on:
BOYS. All on board are sweetly singing—
 Free salvation is the song.
 All the storms, etc.

GIRLS. When we all are safely anchored,
 We will shout—our trials o'er,
BOYS. We will walk about the city,
 And we'll sing for evermore.
 All the storms, etc.

ALL HAIL! THE POWER OF JESUS' NAME.

[From the Golden Censer, page 103.]

All hail! the power of Jesus' name,
 Let angels prostrate fall;
Bring forth the royal diadem,
 And crown him Lord of all.

Ye chosen seed of Israel's race,
  Ye ransom'd from the fall,
Hail him, who saves you by his grace,
  And crown him Lord of all.

Let every kindred, every tribe,
  On this terrestrial ball,
To him all majesty ascribe,
  And crown him Lord of all.

O that with yonder sacred throng
  We at his feet may fall;
We'll join the everlasting song,
  And crown him Lord of all.

AMERICA.

[From the Golden Chain, page 103.]

My country, 'tis of thee,
Sweet land of liberty,
  Of thee I sing;
Land where my fathers died;
Land of the pilgrim's pride;
From every mountain side
  Let freedom ring.

My native country! thee,
Land of the noble free,
  Thy name I love;
I love thy rocks and rills,
Thy woods and templed hills;
My heart with rapture thrills,
  Like that above.

Let music swell the breeze,
And ring from all trees
  Sweet freedom's song;
Let mortal tongues awake;
Let all that breathe partake;
Let rocks their silence break,
  The sound prolong.

A LIGHT IN THE WINDOW.

[From the Golden Censer, page 110.]

There's a light in the window for thee, brother,
There's a light in the window for thee;
A dear one has moved to the mansions above,
There's a light in the window for thee.
A mansion in heaven we see,
And a light in the window for thee.
A mansion in heaven we see,
And a light in the window for thee.

There's a crown, and a robe, and a palm, brother,
When from toil and from care you are free;
The Saviour has gone to prepare you a home,
With a light in the window for thee.
A mansion in heaven we see, etc.

O watch, and be faithful, and pray, brother,
All your journey o'er life's troubled sea,
Tho' afflictions assail you, and storms beat severe,
There's a light in the window for thee.
A mansion in heaven we see, etc.

Then on, perseveringly on, brother,
Till from conflict and suffering free;
Bright angels now beckon you over the stream,
There's a light in the window for thee.
A mansion in heaven we see, etc.

SAVIOUR, LIKE A SHEPHERD LEAD US.

[From the Golden Chain, page 94.]

Saviour, like a shepherd lead us,
Much we need thy tenderest care;
In thy pleasant pastures feed us,
For our use thy folds prepare.
Blessed Jesus, Blessed Jesus,
Thou hast bought us, thine we are;
Blessed Jesus, Blessed Jesus,
Thou hast bought us, thine we are.

We are thine, do thou befriend us,
　Be the Guardian of our way ;
Keep thy flock, from sin defend us,
　Seek us when we go astray.
Blessed Jesus, Blessed Jesus,
　Hear young children when they pray,
Blessed Jesus, Blessed Jesus,
　Hear young children when they pray.

Thou hast promised to receive us,
　Poor and sinful though we be ;
Thou hast mercy to relieve us,
　Grace to cleanse, and power to free.
　　Blessed Jesus,
　Let us early turn to thee.

Early let us seek thy favor,
　Early let us do thy will ;
Blessed Lord and only Saviour,
　With thy love our bosoms fill.
　　Blessed Jesus,
　Thou hast loved us, love us still.

JESUS OUR PILOT.

[From the Golden Censer, page 109.]

Jesus is our Pilot,—
　No one else can guide
Our frail bark in safety,
　O'er life's stormy tide.
When the waves of trouble
　Baffle human skill,
He can always calm them
　With His "Peace, be still!"
　　Jesus is our Pilot—
　　Guided by his hand,
　We shall reach the haven,
　　On the golden strand.

Jesus is our Pilot,—
  Leaning on His arm,
We are safe from danger,
  Safe from fear and harm.
In his strong protection
  Let us ever rest;
Refuge from all sorrow
  On his faithful breast.
            Jesus is our Pilot, etc.

Jesus is our Pilot,—
  Well he knows the way,
From these earthly shadows,
  To the realms of day.
He can find that harbor
  Others seek in vain,
Where as Lord of glory,
  Evermore he'll reign.
            Jesus is our Pilot, etc.

NEVERMORE BE SAD OR WEARY.

[From the Golden Censer, page 107.]

This is not my place of resting,
  Mine's a city yet to come;
Onward to it I'm hasting,
  On to my eternal home.
      Nevermore, nevermore,
        Nevermore be sad or weary,
      Nevermore, nevermore,
        Nevermore to sin again.

In it all is light and glory,
  O'er it shines a nightless day;
Every trace of sin's sad story—
  All the curse has passed away.
      Nevermore, etc.

6

There the Lamb, our Shepherd leads us
   By the streams of life along,
On the freshest pastures feed us,
   Turns our sighing into song.
     Nevermore, etc.

Soon we pass this dreary desert,
   Soon we bid farewell to pain,
Nevermore be sad or weary,
   Nevermore to sin again.
     Nevermore, etc.

BEAUTIFUL LAND OF REST.

[From the Golden Censer, page 104.]

Jerusalem, for ever bright,—
   Beautiful land of rest,
No winter there, nor chill of night,—
   Beautiful land of rest!
The dripping cloud is chased away,
The sun breaks forth in endless day,—
   Jerusalem, Jerusalem,
   The beautiful land of rest.
     Beautiful land, beautiful land,
   Beautiful land of rest,
     Beautiful land, beautiful land,
   Beautiful land of rest.

Jerusalem, for ever free,—
   Beautiful land of rest!
The soul's sweet home of Liberty,—
   Beautiful land of rest!
The gyves of sin, the chains of woe,
The ransomed there will never know,
   Jerusalem, etc.

Jerusalem, for ever dear,—
  Beautiful land of rest!
Thy pearly gates almost appear,—
  Beautiful land of rest!
And when we tread thy lovely shore,
We'll sing the song we've sung before,—
  Jerusalem, etc.

WILL YOU GO?

[From the Golden Censer, page 100.]

We're trav'ling home to heav'n above,
  Will you go? will you go?
To sing the Saviour's dying love,
  Will you go? will you go?
Millions have reached that blest abode,
Anointed kings and priests to God,
And millions now are on the road,
  Will you go? will you go?

We're going to see the bleeding Lamb,
  Will you go? will you go?
In rapturous strains to praise his name,
  Will you go? will you go?
The crown of life we there shall wear,
The conqueror's palms our hands shall bear,
And all the joys of heaven we'll share;
  Will you go? will you go?

Ye weary, heavy-laden, come,
  Will you go? will you go?
In the blest house there still is room,
  Will you go? will you go?
The Lord is waiting to receive,
If thou wilt on him now believe,
He'll give thy troubles, conscience ease,
  Will you go? will you go?

"I NOW BELIEVE."

[From the Golden Censer, page 97.]

There is a fountain filled with blood,
 Drawn from Immanuel's veins;
And sinners plunged beneath that flood,
 Lose all their guilty stains.
 I now believe. I do believe,
  That Jesus died for me;
 That on the cross he shed his blood,
  From sin to set me free.

The dying thief rejoiced to see
 That fountain in his day;
And there may I, though vile as he,
 Wash all my sins away.
 I now believe, I do believe, etc.

Thou dying Lamb, thy precious blood
 Shall never lose its power,
Till all the ransomed Church of God
 Are saved, to sin no more.
 I now believe, I do believe, etc.

E'er since, by faith, I saw the stream
 Thy flowing wounds supply,
Redeeming love has been my theme,
 And shall be, till I die.
 I now believe, I do believe, etc.

Then, in a nobler, sweeter song.
 I'll sing thy power to save;
When this poor, lisping, stammering tongue
 Lies silent in the grave.
 I now believe, I do believe, etc.

TAKE THY CHILDREN HOME.

[From the New Shining Star, page 20.]

Why do we linger?
  We have no resting place,
Rocked by the tempest
  On the ocean's foam.
Why do we linger?
  We are but strangers here;
Father, dear Father,
  Take thy children home.
    Dark and lone our path below,
      By care and sorrow clouded;
    Dreary winds around us blow,
      While onward still we roam.
    Why do we linger?
      We are but strangers here;
    Father, dear Father,
      Take thy children home.

Why do we linger?
  Why cling to earthly joys,
Calling the pilgrim
  From the narrow way?
Trust not their brightness,
  Fleet as the early beam,
Chasing the shadow
  From the brow of day.
    Dark and lone, etc.

There, on thy bosom,
  Sheltered from every storm,
Peace, like a river,
  Shall forever glide:
Laving the vine-tree,
  Cooling the sunny vale,
Bearing the faithful
  On its silver tide.
    Dark and lone, etc.

THE GATHERING.

[From the New Shining Star, page 80.]

We gather, we gather, dear Jesus, to bring
The breathings of love, 'mid the blossoms of Spring;
Our Maker! Redeemer! we gratefully raise ⁻
Our hearts and our voices in hymning thy praise.
    Hallelujah! Hallelujah! Hosanna in the highest!
    Hallelujah! Hallelujah! Hosanna to the Lord!

When stooping to earth from the brightness of heaven,
Thy blood for our ransom so freely was given;
Thou designest to listen while children adored,
With joyful hosannas—the bless'd of the Lord.
    Hallelujah, etc.

Those arms which embraced little children of old,
Still love to encircle the lambs of the fold,
That grace which inviteth the wandering home,
Hath never forbidden the youngest to come.
    Hallelujah, etc.

Hosanna! hosanna! Great Teacher, we raise
Our hearts and our voices in hymning thy praise,
For precepts and promise so graciously given,
For blessings of earth and the glories of heaven.
    Hallelujah, etc.

"MARCHING ON!"

[From the Golden Censer. page 96.]

Marching on! marching on! glad as birds on the wing,
    Come the bright ranks of soldiers from near and from far;
Happy hearts, full of song, 'neath our banners we bring,
    We are soldiers of Zion prepared for the war.
      Marching on! marching on!
      Marching on! marching on! marching on!
      Sound the battle cry! sound the battle cry!
    Marching on! marching on! marching on! marching on!
      Shout the victory, the victory, the victory!

Pressing on! pressing on! to the din of the fray,
   With the firm tread of faith to the battle we go;
'Mid the cheering of angels, our ranks march away,
   With our flags pointing ever right on tow'rds the foe.
      Marching on, etc.

Fighting on! fighting on! in the midst of the strife,
   At the call of our Captain, we draw ev'ry sword;
We are battling for God, we are struggling for life,
   Let us strike ev'ry rebel that fights 'gainst the Lord.
      Marching on, etc.

Singing on! singing on! from the battle we come,
   Ev'ry flag bears a wreath, ev'ry soldier renown;
Heav'nly angels are waiting to welcome us home,
   And the Saviour will give us a robe and a crown.
      Marching on, etc.

ONE PLACE IS VACANT.

[From the Silver Chime, page 73.]

One place is vacant,
   One face is gone,
One form has left us,
   No more to return.
Mournful and sad are the hearts that we bring,
Mournful and sad is the song that we sing.

   One voice is silent,
     One pulse is still,
   One heart no more
     Kind missions fulfill.
      Mournful and sad, etc.

   Dear hands are weary,
     Dear eyes are dim,
   Quick ears are stopped,
     Ne'er to hear us again.
      Mournful and sad, etc.

SING, O YE MOUNTAINS.

[From the New Shining Star, page 48.]

Music, sweet music from angels above,
  Tenderly murmuring low,
Pardon and peace from our Father above,
  Wafted to mortals below,
Send the glad tidings o'er land and o'er sea,
  Joy to the captive proclaim,
Hope to the dying, salvation is free,
  Hope through Immanuel's name.
    Sing, O ye mountains with gladness,
      Joy to the captive proclaim,
      Hope to the dying, salvation is free,
      Hope through Immanuel's name.

Wanderer, return to the portals of light,
  Mourner, no longer repine,
Come to the fountain that sparkles so bright,
  Lave in its waters divine.
Courage, ye fearful, by sorrow oppressed,
  Soldiers, be valiant and brave,
Mariner see, there's a heaven of rest,
  Yonder it smiles on the wave.
    Sing, O ye, etc.

THE POLAR STAR.

[From the New Shining Star, page 96.]

Weary wander o'er the main,
  Seeking for thy home again,
Through the gath'ring mists that rise,
  Veiling thy natal skies;
Look beyond, there's light for thee,
  Streaming o'er the turbid sea,
Softly its smiles tho' distant far,
  The beautiful polar star.

Stranger, on a rocky strand,
    Longing for thy father-land,
Through the gath'ring clouds that rise,
    Veiling thy natal skies,
Look beyond, there's hope for thee,
    Dawning o'er a tranquil sea,
Softly it smiles tho' distant far,
    The beautiful polar star.

Lonely watcher, pale with grief,
    Thou shalt find a sweet relief,
Tho' thy tears unheeded fall,
    Jesus will count them all;
Look beyond, there's joy for thee,
    Breaking o'er a troubled sea,
Softly it smiles tho' distant far,
    The beautiful polar star.

PEACE, BE STILL.

[From the Sabbath School Trumpet, page 73.]

Once, upon the heaving ocean,
    Rode a bark at evening tide,
While the waves, in wild commotion,
    Dashed against the vessel's side,
Jesus, sleeping on a pillow,
    Heeded not the raging billow;
While the winds were all abroad,
    Calmly slept the Son of God.

In that dark and stormy hour,
    Fearful ones awaked their Lord,
Jesus by his sovereign power,
    Calmed the tempest with a word,
On life's dark and restless ocean,
    'Mid the billows wild commotion,
Trembling soul, your Lord is there;
    He will make you still his care.

Jesus knows your silent weeping,
  When before his throne you bow;
Never, never is he sleeping,
  Where he reigns in glory now.
If the world is dark before thee,
  If the billows rolling o'er thee,
All thy soul with terror fill—
  Hear him saying, "Peace—be still!"

OUR HAPPY HOME IN HEAVEN.
[From the New Shining Star, page 58.]

In that world of glory bright,
Where the Saviour is the light,
All is joy, and there's no night,
Nor sin nor sorrow there.
    In our happy home in heaven,
    Where the golden harps are ringing,
    Angels beautiful are singing,
    And all is love and praise.

There the Saviour we shall see,
And our voices then will be,
Tun'd to heaven's minstrelsy,
And sing redeeming love.
    In our happy home, etc.

O, how sweet to think of heav'n,
Happy home to children given:
Here, "by sin and sorrow driv'n,"
There all is perfect rest.
    In our happy home, etc.

Father, guide our steps aright,
May it be our great delight
To live holy in thy sight,
That we may dwell with thee.
    In our happy home, etc.

SOFTLY SHE FADED.

From the Sabbath School Trumpet, page 60.]

Softly she faded, as fades the twilight—
  Sweetly she murmured, "Dear friends adieu!
There is no shadow, all, all is peaceful,
  Bright o'er the river, Heaven is in view."
So 'twas she faded, as fades the twilight,
  So 'twas she murmured, "Dear friends adieu!"

Gently beside her sad tears were falling,
  Softly around her strong arms were thrown,
Fondly she whispered, "Weep not for me,
  My Saviour is here, and I'm going home."
So 'twas she faded, as fades the twilight,
  So 'twas she murmured, "I'm going home."

Joys of the future, home with her Saviour,
  When all is peace forevermore,
Smiling and cheerful, lisped she at parting,
  "Come to the Saviour, Jesus says come."
So 'twas she faded, as fades the twilight,
  So 'twas she murmured, "Jesus says come."

WE COME, WE COME WITH SINGING.

[From the New Shining Star, page 30.]

We come, we come with singing,
  Our happy voices ringing,
    Glad welcome unto all.
We love to meet each other,
Each little friend and brother,
We love to meet our Saviour,
    The dearest friend of all.
      Jesus is here,
      Angels are near;
        Sing, sing, praises sing,
      Jesus is here,
      Angels are near;
        Sing, sing, praises sing.

We come, we come rejoicing,
Our happy voices ringing
  Glad tidings unto all.
We sing, we sing the story,
The sweet, the sweet old story,
How Jesus came from glory,
  And suffered for us all.
    Jesus is here, etc.

Dear Saviour, grant thy blessing
While we, our wants confessing
  Before thee humbly fall.
O, bless us in our praising,
O, help us in our praying,
And let us hear thee speaking
  Within these sacred walls.
    Jesus is here, etc.

GOD OVER ALL.

[From the Sabbath School Trumpet, page 55.]
God in the sunshine, and God in the storm,
God in the night time, and God in the morn;
  God ever near us, to hear when we call,
  God 'neath the star-gems, and God over all.

God in the wild winds, and God in the breeze,
God in the flowers, and God in the trees;
  God ever ready to watch lest we fall,
  God 'neath the heavens, and God over all.

God in the peace time, God in the war,
God in the battles that echo afar,
  God in the good, and the bad, if they call,
  God so forgiving, though God over all.

God in the lightning, and God in the rain,
God in the tempest again and again.
  God in each sorrow he suffers to fall,
  God of the earthworm, and God over all.

CHRISTMAS HYMN.

[From the Sabbath School Trumpet, page 47.]

Shepherds were tending their pastures by night,
Bright o'er the plains shone a heavenly light ;
Angels sent down from the mansions above
Sang the glad message, the message of love.
   Hosanna, hosanna, the Saviour has come,
    Oh, tell the glad news, bring the wanderers home;
   Then, shout the full chorus o'er island and main,
   Till hill-top and valley re-echo again.

Ages have rolled, but that light ne'er grows dim,
Never have ceased the glad tones of that hymn ;
We though but lowly, would joyfully bring
Offerings and praises to Jesus our King.
      Hosanna, etc.

Welcome the morning, now dawning so near,
Glory and joy with its dawning appear ;
Jesus, once dead, is now seated on high.
Reigning in triumph, no more shall he die.
      Hosanna; etc.

THE MORNING LAND.

[From the Sabbath School Trumpet, page 74.]

These many days 'mid storm and rain,
  We've striven 'gainst the tide,
But now the harbor is in view,
  Where we may safely ride,
With anchor weighed, with canvas spread,
  A weary, toiling band,
We hail the breeze that speeds us to
  The glorious morning land.
    The morning land, bright morning land,
      O glorious morning land !
    We soon shall reach thy blissful shore,
      O glorious morning land.

We've wildly tossed upon the deep,
  Our hope a single ray;
But see! the star of morning beams,
  The harbinger of day,
We soon shall furl our tattered sail,
  And press the wished-for land,
Our bark will moor beside thy shore,
  O glorious morning land.
    The morning land, etc.

A heavenly calm shall soothe the waves,
  And bid them hush to sleep;
Eternal sunbeams evermore
  Shall rest upon the deep.
Our bark no more by tempest tossed,
  Shall bear a happy band,
Who rest forever 'mid thy groves,
  O glorious morning land!
    The morning land, etc.

Earth's pilgrims walk thy golden streets,
  In robes of shining white;
Thy city gates are built of pearl,
  And God is all the light.
We've looked from far upon thy shores,
  Our friends have reached the strand;
We soon shall join thy happy throng,
  O glorious morning land!
    The morning land, etc.

SWEETLY NOW, AND SWEETLY EVER.

[From the Sabbath School Trumpet, page 39.]

Sweetly now, and sweetly ever,
  Childhood's voices mingle clear,
As with earnest, true endeavor,
  School they seek with songs of cheer;
    Be their spirits
  Tuned to love and virtue here.

Sweetly now, and sweetly ever,
  Pleasant smiles illume each brow;
Who would wish the ties to sever,
  Which make glad each pupil now;
    May they labor
  Kindness ever more to show.

Sweetly now, and sweetly ever,
  Infant greetings charm each heart;
Be their youthful spirits never
  Crushed neath sorrow's poisoned dart;
    May they never
  From their friends and playmates part.

Sweetly now, and sweetly ever,
  May each youthful voice ascend,
Till the music failing never,
  Shall with heavenly echoes blend;
    May each songster
  Future years in pleasure spend.

WAITING FOR CHRISTMAS.
[From the Sabbath School Trumpet, page 46.]

We are all expecting Christmas,
  World-wide expectation waits
For the merry Christmas coming,
  Thro' the morning's golden gates.
    Merry, merry Christmas, coming,
      The day so full of cheer,
    With joyful songs we'll make it
      The happiest of the year.

Let its rosy morning shower,
  Christmas gifts and Christmas cheer,
Let its sunlight glow upon us,
  As the heaven thro' Christ brought near.
    Merry, merry Christmas, etc.

"Merry Christmas, merry Christmas,"
  Shout the children long ere morn,
Waking, peeping, from the window,
  Waiting for the early dawn.
    Merry, merry Christmas, etc.

We await God's endless Christmas,
  Shines it from his throne above,
Thro' the vista of the ages
  With the steadfast light of love.
    Merry, merry Christmas, etc.

Sing we now our Christmas carol,
  Happy children, ere the morn,
Watching through life's glimmering starlight,
  Waiting for the Christmas dawn.
    Merry, merry Christmas, etc.

I'M A PILGRIM.

[From the Happy Voices, page 209.]

I'm a pilgrim, and I'm a stranger,
  I can tarry, I can tarry but a night.
I'm a pilgrim, and I'm a stranger,
  I can tarry, I can tarry but a night.
Do not detain me, for I am going
To where the fountains are ever flowing

There the glory is ever shining,
Oh my longing heart, my longing heart is there;
Here in this country, so dark and dreary,
I long have wandered, forlorn and weary,
  I'm a pilgrim, and I'm a stranger, etc.

There's the city to which I journey.
My Redeemer, my Redeemer is its light.
There is no sorrow, nor any sighing,
Nor any sin there, nor any dying,
  I'm a pilgrim, and I'm a stranger, etc.

THE HEAVEN ABOVE:

[From the Happy Voices, page 222.]

There's a bright, unfading crown
  In the heaven above,
Sparkling like the dews of morn,
  In the heaven above.
Thousands of children there
That crown of glory wear
Now safe from sin and care,
  In the heaven above.

There's a robe of righteousness
  In the heaven above,
Worn by every heir of grace,
  In the heaven above.
Happy and undefiled,
Many a ransomed child
Shines like the starlight mild,
  In the heaven above.

There's a tuneful harp of gold
  In the heaven above,
Every hand a harp shall hold,
  In the heaven above.
Thousands of children sing
Praise to their Saviour King;
Loud sweep the tuneful string
  In the heaven above.

Would you strike that golden wire
  In the heaven above.
Wear that crown and that attire
  In the heaven above?
Come then to Jesus, come,
Come in your youthful bloom,
Come for there now is room
  In the heaven above.

7

HOMEWARD BOUND.

[From the Happy Voices, page 210.]

Out on an ocean all boundless we ride,
    We're homeward bound, homeward bound;
Tossed on the waves of a rough restless tide,
    We're homeward bound, homeward bound;
Far from the safe quiet harbor we've rode,
Seeking our Father's celestial abode,
Promise of which on us each he bestowed,
    We're homeward bound, homeward bound;

Wildly the storm sweeps us on as it roars,
    We're homeward bound,
Look, yonder lie the bright heavenly shores,
    We're homeward bound.
Steady, O pilot, stand firm at the wheel,
Steady, we soon shall outweather the gale,
Oh how we fly 'neath the loud creaking sail,
    We're homeward bound.

We'll tell the world as we journey along,
    We're homeward bound;
Try to persuade them to enter our throng,
    We're homeward bound.
Come, trembling sinner, forlorn and oppressed,
Join in our number, Oh come and be blest,
Journey with us to the mansions of rest,
    We're homeward bound.

Into the harbor of heaven we glide,
    We're home at last,
Softly we drift on its bright silver tide.
    We're home at last.
Glory to God, all our dangers are o'er,
We stand secure on the glorified shore;
"Glory to God!" we will shout evermore,
    We're home at last.

BEAUTIFUL RIVER.

[From the Happy Voices, page 220.]

Shall we gather at the river
  Where bright angel feet have trod,
With its crystal tide forever,
  Flowing by the throne of God?
    Yes we'll gather at the river,
      The beautiful, the beautiful river,
      Gather with the saints at the river
        That flows by the throne of God.

On the margin of the river,
  Washing up its silver spray,
We will walk and worship ever,
  All the happy golden day.
    Yes we'll gather, etc.

Ere we reach the shining river,
  Lay we every burden down,
Grace our spirits will deliver,
  And provide a robe and crown.
    Yes we'll gather, etc.

At the smiling of the river,
  Mirror of the Saviour's face,
Saints whom death will never sever,
  Lift their songs of saving grace.
    Yes we'll gather, etc.

Soon we'll reach the silver river,
  Soon our pilgrimage will cease,
Soon our happy hearts will quiver
  With the melody of peace.
    Yes we'll gather, etc.

THE SABBATH.

[From the Happy Voices, page 207.]

How sweet is the Sabbath to me,
   The day when the Saviour arose;
'Tis heaven his beauties to see,
   And in his soft arms to repose.
He knows I am weak and defiled,
   My life is but empty and vain.
But if he will make me his child,
   I'll never forsake him again.

This day he invites me to come,
   How kindly he bids me draw near,
He offers me heaven for home,
   And wipes off the penitent tear;
He offers to pardon my sin,
   And keep me from every snare,
To sprinkle and cleanse me within,
   And show me his tenderest care.

THE UPPER FOLD.

[From the Sabbath School Trumpet, page 28.]

In the pastures green of the blessed isles,
   Whose paths are shining gold,
Where the light of life is the Shepherd's smiles,
   Are the lambs of the Upper Fold.
     When we reach that land, that blessed land,
       And receive our crowns of gold,
     We shall dwell in peace with that glorious band,
       Who are safe in the Upper Fold.

Where the lilies blossom in fadeless spring
   And hearts shall ne'er grow old,
Where the glad new song is the song they sing,
   Are the lambs of the Upper Fold.
     When we reach that land, etc.

There are tiny mounds where the hopes of earth
    Were laid beneath the mold,
But the light that paled at the stricken hearth
    Is the joy of the Upper Fold.
      When we reach that land, etc.

Oh! the white stone beareth a new name there
    That ne'er on earth was told,
And the tender Shepherd doth always care
    For the lambs of the Upper Fold.
      When we reach that land, etc.

THE SABBATH MORN.

[From the New Shining Star, page 9.]

The Sabbath morn, the Sabbath morn,
    How lovely bright and clear,
While yonder bell its welcome call
    Is sounding in our ear.
It floats along the fragrant air,
    For nature smiles to day,
Then come, dear children, one and all,
    To Sabbath-school away.
      With hearts and voices cheerily
        We tune our choral lay,
      To Sabbath-school a merry, merry throng,
      We haste, we haste away.

How joyful was the angels' song
    That told the Saviour's birth,
How sweet the tender words he spoke
    To children here on earth,
Then let us seek by humble prayer
    To win his pard'ning love,
And when our day of life is o'er,
    We'll dwell with him above.
      With hearts, etc.

LIVE IN LOVE.

[From the Sabbath School Trumpet, page 45.]

Heaven awakes the gentle strain,
　Live in love, live in love,
Earth repeats the sound again,
　Live, Oh, live in love.
Where the tears of sorrow flow,
And the heart is filled with woe,
Here in accents soft and low,
　Live, Oh, live in love.

Angel voices chant the song,
　Live in love, live in love.
Here below the notes prolong,
　Live, Oh, live in love,
When the heart from care is free,
When the time glides merrily,
That sweet voice still calls for thee,
　Live, Oh, live in love.

SPIRIT VOICES.

[From the New Shining Star, page 8.]

Listen to the roses,
　Listen to the rills,
Listen to the breezes,
　Whispering o'er the hills;
They have each a burden
　For the willing ear,
Ever to the list'ner
　Whispering, "God is near."
　　God is near thee,
　　　Night and day,
　　God will hear thee,
　　　Therefore pray,
　　God is near thee,
　　　Night and day,
　　God will hear thee,
　　　Therefore pray.

Listen to the rain drops,
  Listen to the dew,
Listen to the sunshine,
  Whispering to you;
These are spirit voices,
  Speaking to the heart,
God is ever near thee,
  Wheresoe'er thou art.
    God is near, etc.

JESUS IS OUR SHEPHERD.

[From the New Shining Star, page 36.]

Jesus is our Shepherd,
  On his faithful breast,
Safe from every danger,
  We his flock may rest;
By the cooling streamlet,
  In the valley fair,
He will gently lead us,
  By his tender care.

Jesus is our Shepherd,
  In the dewy mead,
And the verdant meadow,
  He his flock will feed;
He will ne'er desert us,
  To the Tempter's power,
He will kindly cheer us,
  In the darkest hour.

Jesus is our Shepherd,
  He the living way,
From his fold of mercy,
  May we never stray;
When our hearts are wayward,
  When our steps would rove,
Bind us, gentle Shepherd,
  With thy chain of love.

I HAVE A FATHER IN THE PROMISED LAND.

[From the Happy Voices, page 205.]

I have a father in the promised land,
I have a father in the promised land;
　My father calls me, I must go
To meet him in the promised land.
　　I'll away, I'll away to the promised land,
　　I'll away, I'll away to the promised land
　　　My father calls me, I must go
　　To meet him in the promised land.

I have a Saviour in the promised land,
I have a Saviour in the promised land,
　My Saviour calls me, I must go
To meet him in the promised land.
　　I'll away, etc.

I have a crown in the promised land,
I have a crown in the promised land;
　When Jesus calls me, I must go
To wear it in the promised land.
　　I'll away, etc.

I hope to meet you in the promised land,
At Jesus' feet, a joyous band,
We'll praise him in the promised land,
　We'll away, etc.

JOYFULLY, JOYFULLY.

[From the Happy Voices, page 211.]

Joyfully, Joyfully, onward we move
Bound to the land of bright spirits above,
Jesus our Saviour in mercy says come,
Joyfully, joyfully haste to your home.
Soon will our pilgrimage end here below,
Soon to the presence of God we shall go;
Then if to Jesus our hearts have been given,
Joyfully, joyfully rest we in heaven.

Teachers and scholars have passed on before,
Waiting they watch us, approaching the shore,
Singing to cheer us while passing along,
" Joyfully, joyfully haste to your home."
Sounds of sweet music there ravish the ear,
Harps of the blessed, your strains we shall hear
Filling with harmony heaven's high dome,
Joyfully, joyfully, Jesus we come.

Death with his arrow may soon lay us low,
Safe in our Saviour, we fear not the blow,
Jesus hath broken the bars of the tomb,
Joyfully, joyfully will we go home.
Bright will the morn of eternity dawn,
Death shall be conquered, his scepter be gone ;
Over the plains of sweet Canaan we'll roam,
Joyfully, joyfully, safely at home.

HEAVENLY BLISS.

[From the Sabbath School Trumpet, page 56.]

There is a glorious world of light,
    Above the stormy sky ;
Where saints departed, clothed in white,
    Adore the Lord most high.
        Singing glory, glory, glory hallelujah !
        Singing glory, glory, glory hallelujah !

And there in all the sacred songs
    Those heavenly voices raise,
Ten thousand thousand infant tongues
    Unite in perfect praise.
        Singing glory, etc.

Those are the songs that we shall know,
    If Jesus we obey ;
And that the place where we shall go,
    If found in wisdom's ways.
        Singing glory, etc.

EVENING HYMN.

[From the Happy Voices, page 217.]

The day is past and gone,
  The evening shades appear,
Oh may we all remember well
  The night of death draws near.

Lord, keep us safe this night,
  Secure from all our fears;
May angels guard us while we sleep,
  Till morning light appears.

And when we early rise,
  And view th' unwearied sun,
May we set out to win the prize,
  And after glory run.

And when our days are past,
  And we from time remove,
Oh may we in thy bosom rest,
  The bosom of thy love.

SHALL WE MEET BEYOND THE RIVER.

[From the Happy Voices, page 189.]

Shall we meet beyond the river,
  Where the surges cease to roll,
Where in all the bright forever,
  Sorrow ne'er shall press the soul?
    Shall we meet, shall we meet,
    Shall we meet, shall we meet,
      Shall we meet beyond the river,
      Where the surges cease to roll?

Shall we meet in that blest harbor
  When our stormy voyage is o'er;
Shall we meet and cast the anchor
  By the fair celestial shore?
    Shall we meet, etc.

Where the music of the ransomed
　Rolls in harmony around,
And creation swells the chorus
　With its sweet, melodious sound.
　　Shall we meet, etc.

Shall we meet with many a loved one,
　Torn on earth from our embrace?
Shall we listen to their voices,
　And behold them face to face?
　　Shall we meet, etc.

Shall we meet with Christ our Saviour
　When he comes to claim his own?
Shall we hear him bid us welcome,
　And sit down upon his throne?
　　Shall we meet, etc.

INVITATION.

[From the Happy Voices, page 183.]

　From the cross uplifted high,
　Where the Saviour deigns to die,
　What melodious sounds we hear
　Bursting on the ravished ear;
　Love's redeeming work is done;
　Come and welcome sinner, come.

　Sprinkled now with blood the throne,
　Why beneath thy burdens groan?
　On thy pierced body laid,
　Justice owns the ransom paid;
　Bow the knee, and kiss the Son, etc.

　Soon the days of life shall end,
　Lo, I come, your Saviour, Friend,
　Safe your spirits to convey,
　To the realms of endless day—
　Up to my eternal home, etc.

THE NAME OF JESUS.

[From the Happy Voices, page 96.]

How sweet the name of Jesus sounds
  In a believer's ear;
It soothes his sorrows, heals his wounds,
  And drives away his fear.

I do believe, I now believe,
  That Jesus died for me;
And through his blood, his precious blood,
  I shall from sin be free.

It makes the wounded spirit whole,
  And calms the troubled breast;
'Tis manna to the hungry soul,
  And to the weary rest.
    I do believe, etc.

By him my prayers acceptance gain,
  Although with sin defiled;
Satan accuses me in vain,
  And I am owned a child.
    I do believe, etc.

Weak is the effort of my heart,
  And cold my warmest thought;
But when I see thee as thou art,
  I'll praise thee as I ought.
    I do believe, etc.

Till then I would thy love proclaim
  With every fleeting breath;
And may the music of thy name
  Refresh my soul in death.
    . I do believe, etc.

AUTUMN.

[From the Happy Voices, page 190.]

There's a land of peerless beauty,
  And of glory all untold,
Where no shadow ever falleth,
  Where no sunny face grows old;
Where the crystal river floweth
  With the tree upon its banks,
And with love each bosom gloweth
  In the bright celestial ranks.

Oh to reach that clime of gladness,
  Be it all my soul's desire,
Whether joy be mine, or sadness,
  Upward still would I aspire,
Brief the pang my heart that rendeth.
  Brief the joy that swells it here,
But the rapture never endeth
  Of that pure and blessed sphere.

There is Jesus my Redeemer,
  With the many crowns he wears,
And the scars of earthly wounding,
  Precious tokens which he bears;
There the angels, all so glorious,
  In the outer circle stand,
While the souls by faith victorious
  Are a nearer, dearer band.

Then while months and years are taking
  Like a dream their flight away,
If they bring me but the breaking
  Of the one eternal day,
I will not regret their fleetness,
  Nor hold fast to things below,
I will only ask a meetness
  For the bliss to which I go.

MISSIONARY HYMN.

[From the Happy Voices, page 125.]

From Greenland's icy moantains,
    From India's coral strand,
Where Afric's sunny fountains
    Roll down their golden sand;
From many an ancient river,
    From many a palmy plain,
They call us to deliver
    Their land from error's chain.

What tho' the spicy breezes
    Blow soft o'er Ceylon's Isle,
Tho' every prospect pleases,
    And only man is vile;
In vain with lavish kindness
    The gifts of God are strown,
The heathen in his blindness
    Bows down to wood and stone.

Shall we whose souls are lighted
    With wisdom from on high,
Shall we to men benighted
    The lamp of life deny?
Salvation! Oh, salvation!
    The joyful sound proclaim,
Till earth's remotest nation
    Has learned Messiah's name.

Waft, waft, ye winds, his story,
    And you, ye waters, roll,
Till like a sea of glory,
    It spreads from pole to pole;
Till o'er our ransomed nature
    The Lamb, for sinners slain,
Redeemer, King, Creator,
    In bliss returns to reign.

THE GOLDEN RULE.

[From the Sabbath School Trumpet, page 34.]

The golden rule, the golden rule,
O that's the law for me!
Were this the law for all the world,
How happy we should be.
The golden rule, the golden rule,
O that's the law for me!
To do to others as I would
That they should do to me

We love our fathers—mothers too,
Whose love our life attends ;
We love our brothers, sisters too,
Our teachers and our friends.
The golden rule, etc.

The golden rule! then would no war
Be known in any land,
If each one sought the other's good,
And loved the Lord's command.
The golden rule, etc.

Were this the rule, in harmony,
Our lives would pass away,
And none would suffer, none be poor,
And none their trust betray.
The golden rule, etc.

ROCK OF AGES.

[From the Happy Voices, page 183.]

Rock of ages cleft for me,
Let me hide myself in thee ;
Let the water and the blood,
From thy wounded side that flowed,
Be of sin the double cure,
Cleanse me from its guilt and power.

Not the labor of my hands
Can fulfill the law's demands;
Could my zeal no respite know,
Could my tears for ever flow,
All for sin could not atone;
Thou must save and thou alone.

Nothing in my hand I bring,
Simply to thy cross I cling;
Naked, come to thee for dress,
Helpless, look to thee for grace,
Vile, I to the fountain fly;
Wash me, Saviour, or I die.

While I draw this fleeting breath,
When mine eyelids close in death,
When I soar to worlds unknown,
See thee on thy judgment throne,
Rock of ages cleft for me,
Let me hide myself in thee.

PILGRIM BAND.

[From the Golden Chain, page 116.]

Come, little soldiers, join in our band,
March for the kingdom, our promised land,
Fearless of danger, onward we roam,
Jesus our leader is, soon we 'll be home.
    We're a little pilgrim band,
    Guided by a Saviour's hand,
    Soon we'll reach our fatherland,
      No more to roam.

Hark to the voices, bidding us come!
Angels rejoicing, welcome us home;
No more shall sadness or sorrow oppress,
Come, little pilgrim band, there we shall rest.
    We're a little pilgrim band, etc.

Soon we shall never know sorrow more,
But, blest forever, God's love shall share;
Soon we shall see him in his blest home,
Ever still praising him, ages to come.
          We're a little pilgrim band, etc.

HEAVEN IS MY HOME.

[From the Happy Voices, page 184.]

I'm but a stranger here,
    Heaven is my home;
Earth is a desert drear,
    Heaven is my home.
Danger and sorrow stand
Round me on every hand,
Heaven is my fatherland,
    Heaven is my home.

What though the tempest rage,
    Heaven is my home;
Short is my pilgrimage,
    Heaven is my home.
Time's cold and wintry blast
Soon will be overpast,
I shall reach home at last,
    Heaven is my home.

There at my Saviour's side,
    Heaven is my home;
I shall be glorified,
    Heaven is my home.
There are the good and blest,
Those I love most and best,
There too I soon shall rest,
    Heaven is my home.

8

LATTER DAY.

[From the Happy Voices, page 129.]

Glorious things of thee are spoken,
  Zion, city of our God;
He whose word cannot be broken,
  Form'd thee for his own abode;
On the rock of ages founded,
  What can shake thy sure repose?
With salvation's walls surrounded.
  Thou mayest smile at all thy foes.

See the streams of living waters,
  Springing from eternal love,
Well supply thy sons and daughters,
  And all fear of want remove.
Who can faint while such a river
  Ever flows their thirst t' assuage?
Grace which, like the Lord, the giver,
  Never fails from age to age.

Round each habitation hovering,
  See the cloud and fire appear,
For a glory and a covering,
  Showing that the Lord is near.
Thus deriving from their banner
  Light by night and shade by day.
Safe they feed upon the manna
  Which he gives them when they pray.

A BEAUTIFUL HOME.

[From the Happy Voices, page 149.]

There's a beautiful home for thee, brother,
  A home, a home, for thee;
In that land of bliss, where pleasure is.
  There, brother's a home for thee,
    A beautiful home for thee, brother,
    A beautiful home for thee, ;
      In that land of bliss where pleasure is,
      There, brother's a home for thee.

There's a beautiful rest for thee, brother,
 A rest, a rest for thee ;
In those mansions above where all is love,
 There, brother's a rest for thee.
  A beautiful rest for thee, etc.

There's a beautiful crown for thee, brother,
 A crown, a crown for thee,
When the battle is done, and the victory won,
 Our Saviour will give it to thee.
  A beautiful crown for thee, etc.

There's a beautiful robe for thee, brother,
 A robe, a robe for thee ;
A robe of white, so pure and bright,
 A glorious robe for thee.
  A beautiful robe for thee, etc.

Wilt seek that beautiful home, brother,
 That home, that home above ;
In that land of light, where all is bright,
 That land where all is love?
  A beautiful home for thee, etc.

THE ANGEL'S SONG.

[From the Golden Chain, page 114.]

There's a song the angels sing,
 And its notes with rapture ring,
Round the throne whose radiance fills the heavens above,
 Shepherds heard the distant strain,
 Watching on Judea's plain,
"Glory be to God, glory be to God, glory be to God, to men
  be peace and love."
  Thro' the earth and thro' the sky,
  Let the anthem ever fly,
  "Glory be to God again,
  Peace on earth, good will to men."

'Tis a song for children too;
To the Saviour 'tis their due;
Let its grateful notes ascend to him again;
Join with angels in their song,
And the heavenly strain prolong,
"Glory be to God, good will and peace to men."
Through the earth, etc.

Soon around that throne may we
With those happy angels be,
Striking harps to strains that nevermore shall cease;
Mingling love with loftiest praise,
Still the chorus there we'll raise,
"Glory oe to God, to men good will and peace."
Through the earth, etc.

MARCHING ALONG.

[From the Golden Chain, page 112.]

The children are gath'ring from near and from far,
The trumpet is sounding the call for the war,
The conflict is raging, 't will be fearful and long,
We'll gird on our armor, and be marching along.
Marching along, we are marching along,
Gird on the armor, and be marching along,
The conflict is raging, 't will be fearful and long,
Then gird on the armor, and be marching along.

The foe is before us, in battle array,
But let us not waver, nor turn from the way,
The Lord is our strength, be this ever our song,
With courage and faith we are marching along.
Marching along, etc.

We 've listed for life, and will camp on the field,
With Christ as our Captain, we never will yield;
The "sword of the Spirit," both trusty and strong,
We'll hold in our hands as we're marching along.
Marching along, etc.

Through conflicts and trials our crowns we must win,
For here we contend 'gainst temptation and sin ;
But one thing assures us, we cannot go wrong,
If trusting our Saviour, while marching along.
    Marching along, etc. _

A FRIEND THAT'S EVER NEAR.

[From the Golden Chain, page 106.]

Though the days are dark with trouble,
  And thy heart is filled with fear,
There is one that sees thee ever,
  And will hold thee near and dear.
Cheerful hearts and smiling faces
  Often make thee happy here,
Yet no one was e'er so happy
  But sometimes the clouds appear.
    There's a friend that's ever near, never fear,
    He is ever near, never, never fear.

All thy prospects will seem brighter
  When the shadow leaves the heart,
And the steps of time beat lighter,
  When the gloomy clouds depart.
Many days have dawned serenely,
  While the birds sang with delight,
But the skies were dark and gloomy
  Ere the sun had reached its height.
    There's a friend, etc.

Soon will dawn a brighter morning,
  On a blessed, tranquil shore ;
Sighs will then give place to singing,
  Tears to bliss forevermore.
Thou shalt see a world of glory,
  And eternal joy and bliss ;
Let not then thy soul be moaning
  O'er the woes and cares of this.
    There's a friend, etc.

MORNING LIGHT.

[From the Happy Voices, page 125.]

The morning light is breaking,
    The darkness disappears.
The sons of earth are waking
    To penitential tears ;
Each breeze that sweeps the ocean
    Brings tidings from afar,
Of nations in commotion,
    Prepared for Zion's war.

See heathen nations bending
    Before the God we love,
And thousand hearts ascending
    In gratitude above ;
While sinners now confessing
    The Gospel call obey,
And seek the Saviour's blessing,
    A nation in a day.

Blest river of salvation
    Pursue thy onward way,
Flow thou to every nation,
    Nor in thy richness stay ;
Stay not till all the lowly,
    Triumphant reach their home ;
Stay not till all the holy
    Proclaim, "The Lord has come."

LET THEM COME UNTO ME.

[From the Sabbath School Trumpet, page 20.]

The merciful Saviour, so loving and meek,
    Was heard as men crowded his wonders to see,
And children were kept from his presence to speak,
    And say, "Let the little ones come unto me."
        Come unto me, come unto me,
        Let the little ones come unto me.

That voice from the world has its music withdrawn,
    Its heavenly light, that compassionate eye,
But still in the Sabbath school smileth he on,
    And here in his accents yet lingers the cry:
      "Come unto me," etc.

If idleness come with this troublesome throng,
    If vanity scatter her snares in the way,
To keep us from Jesus in lesson or song,
    We hear him above their forbidding still say:
    "Come unto me," etc.

COME AND BE HAPPY.

[From the Sabbath School Trumpet, page 15.]
    Come and be happy, in life's early spring,
    Virtue true bliss shall bring.
    Nothing so lovely in age or in youth,
    Joy dwells alone with truth.
        Vice is thy bane;
        Wisdom shall reign,
        All her ways pleasantness,
        And all her paths are peace.

Come and be happy, in life's sunny morn,
Goodness thy youth adorn.
Seek for it early, and so shalt thou find
Bliss in thy heart enshrined.
        Pleasures of sin
        Only begin
        Ere their joys turn to pain,
        And ne'er return again.

Come and be happy, and lay up in store
Pleasures forevermore.
Seek thy enjoyment in pleasing the Lord,
Strive for his great reward.
        Ere thou shalt own
        Joys all have flown,
        Bid thy heart meekly bow,
        God cries, "Remember now."

HOW SWEET 'TIS TO MEET.

[From the Sabbath School Trumpet, page 9.]

How sweet 'tis to meet with companions so dear,
And pray to our Saviour who always is near;
To pray that in mercy there yet may be room,
In those blessed realms, our eternal sweet home.
 Home! home! that blessed home;
  O take us in mercy to that blessed home.

Sweet bonds of this school, that unite us in peace,
And thrice blessed Jesus, whose love cannot cease;
Tho' oft from thy presence we're tempted to roam,
We long to behold thee in glory at home.
 Home, home, that blessed home, etc.

Then, Saviour, dear Saviour, O help us to pray,
And keep us, oh! keep us from sin's dreary way;
Oh guide us, in mercy, and aid us to come,
And find even now a sweet foretaste of home.
 Home, home, that blessed home, etc.

HERE AND YONDER.

[From the Sabbath School Trumpet, page 8.]

 Here, we are but straying pilgrims,
  Here, our path is often dim,
 But to cheer us on our journey,
  Still we sing this wayside hymn:
   Yonder over the rolling river,
    Where the shining mansions rise,
   Soon will be our home forever,
   And the smile of the blessed giver
    Gladden all our longing eyes.

 Here, our feet are often weary,
  On the hills that throng our way,
 Here the tempest darkly gathers,
  But our hearts within us say:
   Yonder over the rolling river, etc.

Here, our souls are often fearful,
   Of the pilgrim's lurking foe ;
But the Lord is our Defender,
   And he tells us we may know ;
      Yonder over the rolling river, etc.

Here, our shadowed homes are transient,
   And we meet the stranger's frown,
So we'll sing with joy while going,
   E'en to death's dark billow down :
      Yonder over the rolling river, etc.

HARWELL.

[From the Happy Voices, page 122.]

Hark ! ten thousand harps and voices
   Sound the notes of praise above ;
Jesus reigns, and heaven rejoices,
   Jesus reigns the God of love.
See, he sits on yonder throne,
Jesus rules the world alone.
      Hallelujah ! Hallelujah !
      Hallelujah ! Amen.

Jesus hail ! whose glory brightens
   All above and gives it worth ;
Lord of life, thy smile enlightens,
   Cheers and charms thy saints on earth ;
When we think of love like thine,
Lord, we own it love divine.
      Hallelujah, etc.

King of glory, reign for ever—
   Thine an everlasting crown ;
Nothing from thy love shall sever
   Those whom thou hast made thine own ;
Happy objects of thy grace,
Destined to behold thy face.
      Hallelujah, etc.

Saviour, hasten thine appearing;
  Bring, oh bring the glorious day,
When, the awful summons hearing,
  Heaven and earth shall pass away;
Then with golden harps we'll sing
"Glory, glory to our King."
    Hallelujah, etc.

FLEE TO YOUR MOUNTAIN.

Flee as a bird to your mountain,
  Thou who art weary of sin;
Go to the clear flowing fountain,
  Where you may wash and be clean;
Fly for the avenger is near thee;
  Call, and the Saviour will hear thee;
He on his bosom will bear thee,
  O thou, who art weary of sin,
  O thou, who art weary of sin.

He will protect thee forever,
  Wipe every sad falling tear,
He will forsake thee, O never,
  Cherished so tenderly there;
Haste, then, the hours now are flying,
  Spend not the moments in sighing;
Cease from your sorrow and crying,
  The Saviour will wipe ev'ry tear,
  The Saviour will wipe ev'ry tear.

Come, then, to Jesus thy Saviour,
  He will redeem thee from sin;
Bless with a sense of his favor,
  Make thee all glorious within;
Call, for the Saviour is near thee,
  Waiting in mercy to hear thee,
And by his presence to cheer thee,
  O thou, who art weary of sin,
  O thou, who art weary of sin.

STAND UP FOR JESUS.

[From the Golden Chain, page 105.]

Stand up!—stand up for Jesus!
　Ye soldiers of the cross;
Lift high his royal banner,
　It must not suffer loss;
From victory unto victory
　His army shall be led,
Till every foe is vanquished,
　And Christ is Lord indeed.

Stand up!—stand up for Jesus!
　The trumpet call obey;
Forth to the mighty conflict
　In this his glorious day;
"Ye are the men now serve him,"
　Against unnumbered foes;
Your courage rise with danger,
　And strength to strength oppose.

Stand up!—stand up for Jesus!
　Stand in his strength alone;
The arm of flesh will fail you—
　Ye dare not trust your own;
Put on the Gospel armor,
　And, watching unto prayer,
Where duty calls or danger
　Be never wanting there.

Stand up!—stand up for Jesus!
　The strife will not be long;
This day the noise of battle,
　The next the victor's song;
To him that overcometh,
　A crown of life shall be;
He with the King of glory
　Shall reign eternally.

WATCHMAN, TELL ME.

[From the Golden Censer, page 123.]

Watchman, tell me, does the morning
　Of fair Zion's glory dawn?
Have the signs that mark its coming
　·Yet upon thy pathway shone?
Pilgrim, yes, arise, look round thee;
　Light is breaking in the skies;
Gird thy bridal robes around thee,
　Morning dawns, arise, arise !

Watchman, see, the light is beaming,
　Brighter still upon the way;
Signs through all the earth are gleaming,
　Omens of the coming day
When the Jubal trumpet sounding,
　Shall awake from earth and sea,
And the saints of God now sleeping,
　Clad in immortality.

Watchman, hail, the light ascending,
　Of the grand Sabbatic year;
All with voices loud proclaiming
　That the kingdom's very near;
Pilgrim, yes, I see just yonder,
　Canaan's glorious heights arise,
Salem too appears in grandeur,
　Towering 'neath its sun-lit skies.

Watchman, in the golden city,
　Seated on His jasper throne,
Zion's king enthroned in beauty,
　Reigns in peace from zone to zone;
There on sun-lit hills and mountains,
　Golden beams serenely glow;
Purling streams and crystal fountains,
　On whose banks sweet flow'rets blow.

Watchman, see, the land is nearing,
  With its vernal fruits and flowers,
On just yonder, O how cheering
  Bloom forever Eden's bowers!
Hark! the choral strains are ringing,
  Wafted on the balmy air,
See the millions, hear them singing,
  Soon the pilgrim will be there.

SABBATH MORNING HYMN.

[From the Golden Chain, page 105.]

The rosy light is dawning
  Upon the mountain's brow,
It is the Sabbath morning,
  Arise and pay thy vow.
Lift up thy voice to heaven
  In sacred praise and prayer,
While unto thee is given
  The light of life to share.

The landscape lately shrouded
  By evening's paler ray,
Smiles beauteous and unclouded
  Before the eye of day.
So let our souls benighted
  Too long in folly's shade,
Lord, by thy smile be lighted
  To joys that never fade.

O see those waters streaming
  In crystal purity,
While earth with verdure teeming,
  Gives rapture to the eye.
Let rivers of salvation
  In larger currents flow,
Till every tribe and nation
  Their healing virtues know.

GLORY TO GOD IN THE HIGHEST.

[From the Golden Censer, page 116.]

Glory to God in the highest!
  Glory to God, Glory to God,
Glory to God in the highest!
  Shall be our song to-day;
Another year's rich mercies prove
His ceaseless care and boundless love;
So let our loudest voices raise,
Our Anniversary song of praise.
  Glory to God in the highest
  Glory to God in the highest!
  Glory, glory, glory, glory,
  Glory be to God on high!
    God on hgh!

Glory to God in the highest!
  Shall be our song to-day;
The song that woke the glorious morn
When David's greater son was born,
Sung by an heavenly host, and we
Would join the angelic company.
  Glory to God in the highest, etc.

Glory to God in the highest!
  Shall be our song to-day,
And while we with the angels sing;
Gifts with the wise men let us bring
Unto the Babe of Bethlehem,
And offer our young hearts to him.
  Glory to God in the highest, etc.

Glory to God in the highest!
  Shall be our song to-day.
O, may we, an unbroken band,
Around the throne of Jesus stand,
And there with angels and the throng
Of his redeemed ones, join the song.
  Glory to God in the highest, etc.

LITTLE PILGRIMS.

[From the Sabbath School Trumpet, page 108.]

Little pilgrim, stay and tell us,
 Whither, whither do ye go?
Treading lightly, daily, nightly,
 Murmuring music soft and low.
Treading lightly, daily, nightly,
 Murmuring music, on we go;
Traveling to our home in heaven,
 Blessed home by Jesus given.
  Daily, nightly, treading lightly,
   Glad and happy on we go;
  Treading lightly, daily, nightly,
   Murmuring music soft and low.

Little pilgrims, stay and tell us,
 Of the home to which you go;
Grief and sighing, pain and dying,
 There as here do children know?
Grief and sighing, pain and dying,
 Little children never know,
In that happy home in heaven,
 Blessed home by Jesus given.
  Grief and sighing, pain and dying,
   No one there shall ever know;
  In that happy home in heaven,
   Blessed home by Jesus given.

Little pilgrims, stay and tell us,
 May we go along with you?
Earth is dreary, we are weary,
 We would find that heaven too,
Earth is dreary, come ye weary,
 There is room enough for you;
In that happy home in heaven,
 Blessed home by Jesus given.
  Earth is dreary, come ye weary,
   Share our joys forever new;
  In that happy home in heaven,
   Blessed home by Jesus given.

OPENING HYMN.

[From the Sabbath School Trumpet, page 114.]

We meet again in gladness,
  And thankful voices raise;
To God our heavenly Father,
  We'll tune our grateful praise.
'Tis his kind hand hath kept us
  Thro' every changing year;
His love it is that brings us
  With songs, to worship here,

We'll thank him for the Sabbath,
  This day of holy rest;
And for the blessed Bible,
  The book that we love best;
For Sabbath schools and teachers,
  To us so kindly given,
To guide us in the pathway
  That leads to joys in heaven.

We'll thank him for our country,
  The land our fathers trod;
For liberty of conscience,
  And right to worship God.
We pray for our loved country,
  That civil war may cease;
And liberty and union
  Prevail, and still increase.

Soon may thy gracious sceptre,
  Extend to every land,
And all, as willing subjects,
  Submit to thy command;
Send forth the glorious tidings,
  And hasten on the day
When every isle and nation,
  Shall own Messiah's sway.

WE'RE GOING HOME.

[From the Sabbath School Trumpet, page 23.]

We're going to a happy home;
  We're going home, we're going home,
And see our Saviour face to face;
  We're going home, we're going home.
To join with those before us gone,
  We're going home, we're going home.
To clasp again in fond embrace
The loved ones of that happy place,
  We're going home, we're going home.

Oh, peaceful is that blessed shore—
  We're going home, we're going home,
And pain and death forever cease,
  We're going home, we're going home.
Where ills of life afflict no more;
  We're going home, we're going home.
The sorrowing pilgrim finds release,
The weary rest in perfect peace,
  We're going home, we're going home.

We're going! O what joys arise!
  We're going home, we're going home.
We'll gladly shout when death is nigh,
  We're going home, we're going home.
Hopes of that blissful paradise;
  We're going home, we're going home.
Then let our feeble bodies die,
We have a mansion in the sky;
  We're going home, we're going home.

COME, BROTHERS, ONWARD.

[From the Sabbath School Trumpet, page 21.]

Come, brothers, onward,
  Come, come, without delay,
Jesus, the Saviour cries,
  "I am the way."

9

Come, join the happy throng,
  We're hast'ning on to heaven,
  Where endless praise is given,
In one glad song.

Come. venture boldly,
  Bid worldly thoughts adieu,
Trust his Almighty grace,
  Faithful and true.
No more in darkness roam,
  But Jesus' aid implore;
  He calls from yonder shore,
"Children, come home."

Soon will be ended
  Our warfare here begun;
Fight till the prize is gained,
  The victory won.
Then with the happy blest,
  In yonder heavenly home,
  Where all the loved ones come,
Safely we'll rest.

THERE'S JOY IN JESUS' LOVE.

[From the Sabbath School Trumpet, page 27.]

We come this day to praise
  Our Saviour and our God,
To him our songs we raise,
  Who bought us with his blood.
From sin's dark waste of tears,
  We raise our thoughts above,
And sing despite our fears,
  There's joy in Jesus' love.
    There's joy in Jesus' love,
      To all who faithful live,
    There's joy in Jesus' love,
      That nothing else can give.

Our hope is fixed alone
  On him whom we adore;
For blessings all his own,
  We'll praise him evermore.
His care that bids us live,
  His grace that points above,
His word whose pages give,
  The joy of Jesus' love.
    There's joy in Jesus' love, etc.

With ever tender care
  Our little ones are led,
The joys of heaven to share
  With Christ their living head.
We thank our heavenly King,
  That mercy from above,
Has taught our lambs to sing,
  There's joy in Jesus' love.
    There's joy in Jesus' love, etc.

THE UNION BAND.

[From the Sabbath School Trumpet, page 24.]

O we're a band of brethren dear,
  Who will join this happy band?
Who live as pilgrim strangers here,
  Who will join this happy band?
    Hallelujah, hallelujah,
    We will join this happy band,
      Singing Hallelujah, hallelujah,
    We will join this happy band.

The prophets and apostles too,
  Once belonged to this happy band,
And all God's children here below,
  All have joined this happy band.
    Hallelujah, etc.

Let no contention e'er divide,
  Members of this happy band
But firm united side by side,
  Thro' this life together stand
    Hallelujah, etc.

And when death comes, as come it must,
  To divide this happy band,
The links will not return to dust,
  They will shine at God's right hand.
    Hallelujah, etc.

NO SORROW THERE.

[From the Happy Voices, page 217.]

Oh sing to me of heaven
  When I am called to die;
Sing songs of holy ecstacy
  To waft my soul on high.
    There'll be no sorrow there,
    There'll be no sorrow there;
      In heaven above where all is love,
    There'll be no sorrow there.

When cold and sluggish drops
  Roll off my marble brow,
Break forth in songs of joyfulness,
  Let heaven begin below.
    There'll be no sorrow there, etc.

Then to my raptured ear
  Let one sweet song be given,
Let music charm me last on earth,
  And greet me first in heaven.
    There'll be no sorrow there, etc.

When round my senseless clay
  Assemble those I love.
Then sing of heaven, delightful heaven,
  My glorious home above.
    There'll be no sorrow there, etc.

THE HOME OF THE ANGELS.

[From the Sabbath School Trumpet, page 40.]

There's a rest in the home of the angels,
  That home by and by will be ours,
When gladly we turn from the pathway
  That's strewn with earth's fairest of flowers.
No shadow of sorrow or sadness
  Can dim the bright light of that sky;
But ever in anthems of gladness
  We'll join with the blest by and by,
  We'll join with the blest by and by.

We shall rest in the home of the angels,
  The sky may be covered with gloom,
A bright star of promise is beaming
  Beyond the dark shades of the tomb.
Tho' thorny the way be and dreary,
  And tears may bedim every eye,
The rest for the careworn and weary
  Will ever be ours by and by,
  Will ever be ours by and by.

O, that beautiful home of the angels,
  Is radiant with unfading morn,
And hence to its heavenly mansions
  How many dear loved ones have gone;
They've hastened to glory before us,
  To dwell with the angels on high,
And there with the sanctified legions
  We'll meet them with joy by and by,
  We'll meet them with joy by and by.

NEW YEAR'S HYMN.

[From the Sabbath School Trumpet, page 51.]

  Another year has passed away
    In silence gone forever;
  Yet memory shall bid it stay,
    Its acts shall perish never!

Our prayers and praise this day we raise
  To him whom all things giveth,
That by his side we may abide,
  Where he forever liveth.

And has it passed away unblessed?
  Have all its hours been wasted?
Not all, yet far too much in rest
  The joys of God we've tasted.
    Our prayers and praise, etc.

And does the lesson we receive,
  Bid us to faint in sorrow?
Oh no! it bids us look and live,
  And hope from faith to borrow.
    Our prayers and praise, etc.

And forward in the coming year,
  We'll strive to win the blessing;
And though in darkness, never fear
  The love of Christ possessing.
    Our prayers and praise, etc.

ARE WE FAITHFUL?

[From the Sabbath School Trumpet, page 106.]

Brothers in the Sabbath school,
  Are we faithful, are we true—
Do we love our Saviour's rule?
  Are we prompt to speak and do?
Now again time's ceaseless hand
  Points us to the passing years—
Points us to that unknown land,
  Bright with hopes, or dim with fears.
    Onward, upward, press along,
      Bear the cross to win the prize;
    Christ shall be our theme, our song,
      When we reach those blissful skies.

Sisters in the Sabbath school,
  Are its busy hours well spent?
Do we love our Saviour's rule?
  With our works is he content?
Let us strive that he may smile
  On our labor as we meet—
Looking upward all the while,
  Upward to the mercy seat.
    Onward, upward, etc.

Teachers, is the work complete—
  All our last year's labor done?
Shall we, when above we meet,
  Find our crown of victory won?
Scholars, are our hearts all right?
  Love we all our Saviour's voice?
Is his favor our delight—
  Have we made His path our choice?
    Onward, upward, etc.

LITTLE SCHOOLMATES.

[From the Sabbath School Trumpet, page 85.]

Little schoolmates can you tell
Who has kept us safe and well,
  Thro' the watches of the night,
  Till the morning light?
Yes; it is our God doth keep
Little children while they sleep;
  He has kept us safe from harm,
  By his powerful arm.

Can you tell who gives us food,
Clothes, and home, and parents good,
  Schoolmates dear, and teachers kind,
  Books and active mind?
Yes; our heavenly Father's care
Gives us all we eat and wear;
  All our books and all our friends,
  God in kindness sends.

O, then, let us thankful be,
For his mercies large and free;
   Every morning let us raise,
   High our song of praise;
Praise him for these happy hours,
Praise him for our varied powers,
   Praise him, every heart and voice,
   While we all rejoice.

THERE IS A BEAUTIFUL WORLD.

[From the Sabbath School Trumpet, page 69.]

There is a beautiful world,
   Where saints and angels sing;
A world where peace and pleasure reigns,
   And heavenly praises ring.
     We'll be there, we'll be there,
     Yes, we'll be there,
   Palms of victory, crowns of glory,
     We all shall wear.

There is a beautiful world,
   Where sorrow never comes;
A world where tears shall never fall,
   In sighing for our home.
     We'll be there, etc.

There is a beautiful world,
   Unseen to mortal sight;
And darkness never enters there—
   That home is fair and bright.
     We'll be there, etc.

There is a beautiful world,
   Of harmony and love; .
Oh! may we safely enter there,
   And dwell with God above.
     We'll be there, etc.

THE SCHOLAR'S PRAYER.

[From the Sabbath School Trumpet, page 89.]

Our heavenly Father hear us,
  Dear Saviour deign to hear,
O, be thy presence near us,
  And let thy face appear,
We have met to praise thee now,
  And sing thy dying love,
We've met to read thy holy word,
  And learn of thee above.
    Our heavenly Father hear us,
      Dear Saviour deign to hear,
    O, be thy presence near us,
      And let thy face appear.

We come to thee as children,
  We come that we may know,
Thy teachings, ere we further,
  On life's rough journey go;
Give us heart-felt faith in prayer,
  And give us earnest zeal,
That we in all may be sincere,
  And what we ask for—feel.
    Our heavenly Father hear us, etc.

Life's cares will soon o'ertake us,
  Life's sorrows soon oppress,
But thou wilt walk before us,
  And every effort bless;
When the close of life shall come,
  All ready may we be
To hear thy gently bidding voice,
  " Ye blessed, come to me."
    Our heavenly Father hear us, etc.

BATTLING FOR THE LORD.

[From the Singing Pilgrim, page 25.]

We've listed in a holy war,
    Battling for the Lord!
Eternal life, eternal joy,
    Battling for the Lord!

We'll work till Jesus comes,
    We'll work till Jesus comes,
We'll work tell Jesus comes,
    And then we'll rest at home.

Under our Captain, Jesus Christ,
    Battling for the Lord!
We've listed for this mortal life,
    Battling for the Lord!
        We'll work, etc.

We'll fight against the powers of sin,
    Battling for the Lord!
In favor of our heavenly King,
    Battling for the Lord!
        We'll work, etc.

And when our warfare here is o'er,
    Battling for the Lord!
This strife we'll leave, and war no more,
    Battling for the Lord!
        We'll work, etc.

Our friends and kindred there we'll meet,
    On the heavenly shore!
And ground our arms at Jesus' feet,
    On the heavenly shore!
        We'll work, etc.

Home, home, sweet, sweet home
Prepare me, dear Saviour, for glory, my home.

OUR SAVIOUR'S COMMAND.

[From the Singing Pilgrim, page 16.]

O'er the portals of mercy these words are inscribed,
    And written in letters of gold;
The wayfaring man may behold them afar,
    And knock at the heavenly fold.

    Knock, knock, knock, 't is the Saviour's command,
      Knock at the portals above;
    Knock, knock, knock, 't is the Saviour's command,
      Enter into the mansion of love.

O, ye weary, draw nigh, 't is the place of repose;
    Ye footsore your journeyings cease;
Ye toilworn with labor, new vigor put on,
    And knock at the portals of peace.

    Knock, knock, knock, etc.

All ye mourners, believing, in confidence come;
    Ye desolate, haste to look up;
Ye troubled in heart be resigned to his word,
    And knock at the portals of hope.

    Knock, knock, knock, etc.

And ye sinners, O come! there's a palace for you,
    Prepared by the Builder above;
Approach with your burden, in meekness submit,
    And knock at the portals of love.

    Knock, knock, knock, etc.

They're all waiting within, and the feast is prepared.
    What folly to tarry and wait!
Let every one come in obedient haste,
    And knock at the heavenly gate.

    Knock, knock, knock, etc.

JESUS WAITS FOR THEE.

[From the Singing Pilgrim, page 14.]

Come, come to Jesus!
  He waits to welcome thee,
O Wand'rer! eagerly;
  Come, come to Jesus!

Come, come to Jesus!
  He waits to ransom thee,
O Slave! eternally;
  Come, come to Jesus!

Come, come to Jesus!
  He waits to lighten thee,
O Burdened! graciously;
  Come, come to Jesus!

Come, come to Jesus!
  He waits to give to thee,
O Blind! a vision free;
  Come, come to Jesus!

Come, come to Jesus!
  He waits to shelter thee,
O Weary! blessedly;
  Come, come to Jesus!

Come, come to Jesus!
  He waits to carry thee,
O Lamb! so lovingly;
  Come, come to Jesus!

YOUR MISSION.

[From Musical Leaves, page 90.]

If you can not on the ocean,
  Sail among the swiftest fleet,
Rocking on the highest billows,
  Laughing at the storms you meet,
You can stand among the sailors,
  Anchored yet within the bay;
You can lend a hand to help them,
  As they launch their boat away.

If you are too weak to journey
  Up the mountain, steep and high,
You can stand within the valley,
  While the multitudes go by;
You can chant in happy measure,
  As they slowly pass along;
Though they may forget the singer,
  They will not forget the song.

If you have not gold and silver
  Ever ready to command;
If you can not t'ward the needy
  Reach an ever open hand;
You can visit the afflicted,
  O'er the erring you can weep;
You can be a true disciple
  Sitting at the Saviour's feet.

If you can not in the harvest
  Garner up the richest sheaves,
Many a grain both ripe and golden
  Will the careless reapers leave;
Go and glean among the briers,
  Growing rank against the wall,
For it may be that their shadow,
  Hides the heaviest wheat of all.

If you.cannot in the conflict
  Prove yourself a soldier true —
If, where fire and smoke are thickest,
  There's no work for you to do;
When the battle-field is silent,
  You can go with careful tread,
You can bear away the wounded,
  You can cover up the dead.

Do not, then, stand idly waiting,
  For some greater work to do;
Fortune is a lazy goddess —
  She will never come to you.
Go and toil in any vineyard,
  Do not fear to do or dare;
If you want a field of labor,
  You can find it any where.

I WILL SING FOR JESUS.

[From the Singing Pilgrim, page 89.]

I will sing for Jesus,
  With his blood he bought me;
And all along my pilgrim way
  His loving hand has brought me.

    O! help me sing for Jesus,
      Help me tell the story
    Of him who did redeem us,
      The Lord of life and glory.

Can there overtake me
  Any dark disaster,
While I sing for Jesus,
  My blessed, blessed Master?
    O! help me sing for Jesus, etc.

I will sing for Jesus!
  His name alone prevailing,
Shall be my sweetest music,
    When heart and flesh are failing.

      O! help me sing for Jesus, etc.

Still I'll sing for Jesus!
  O! how will I adore him,
Among the cloud of witnesses,
    Who cast their crowns before him.

     O help me sing for Jesus, etc.

LOVE NOT THE WORLD.

[From the Singing Pilgrim, page 44.]

Why should we covet the joy of a day,
Things that will fade in a moment away;
Toiling for wealth and its honors to gain,
Why are we living for trifles so vain.

    Trust not the world in its beauty arrayed,
    Though at our feet all its treasures be laid;
    What would it profit its wealth to control?
    What can we give in exchange for the soul!

We have no promise that fame will endure;
Splendor will never our pardon secure;
Gold can not brighten the gloom of the grave;
Only the merits of Jesus can save.

    Trust not the world, etc.

Blessed are they who are lowly in heart;
They who, like Mary, have chosen their part;
Learning of Jesus, their Master above,
Lessons of patience, of meekness, and love.

    Trust not the world, etc.

LOVE AT HOME.

[From the Happy Voices, page 141.]

There is beauty all around,
   When there's love at home,
There's joy in every sound,
   When there's love at home.
Peace and plenty here abide,
Smiling sweet on every side,
Time doth softly, sweetly glide,
  . When there's love at home.
Love at home, love at home;
   Time doth softly, sweetly glide,
When there's love at home.

In the cottage there is joy,
   When there's love at home;
Hate and envy ne'er annoy,
   When there's love at home.
Roses blossom 'neath our feet,
All the earth's a garden sweet,
Making life a bliss complete,
  . When there's love at home.

Kindly heaven smiles above,
   When there's love at home;
All the earth is filled with love,
   When there's love at home.
Sweeter sings the brooklet by,
Brighter beams the azure sky;
Oh, there's One who smiles on high,
   When there's love at home.

Jesus, show thy mercy mine;
   Then there's love at home;
Sweetly whisper, I am thine,
   Then there's love at home.
Source of love, thy cheering light
Far exceeds the sun so bright —
Can dispel the gloom of night;
   Then there's love at home.

I ALWAYS GO TO JESUS.

[From the Sunday School Times.]

I always go to Jesus,
    When troubled or distressed;
I always find a refuge
    Upon his loving breast.
I tell him all my trials,
    I tell him all my grief;
And while my lips are speaking,
    He gives my heart relief.

When full of dread forebodings,
    And flowing o'er with tears,
He calms away my sorrows,
    And hushes all my fears.
He comprehends my weakness,
    The peril I am in,
And he supplies the armor
    I need to vanquish sin.

When those are cold and faithless,
    Who once were fond and true,
With careless hearts forsaking
    The old friends for the new.
I turn to him whose friendship
    Knows neither change nor end,
I always find in Jesus
    An ever faithful Friend.

I always go to Jesus;
    No matter when or where,
I seek his gracious presence,
    I'm sure to find him there.
In times of joy or sorrow,
    Whate'er my need may be,
I always *go* to Jesus,
    And Jesus *comes* to me.

                JOSEPHINE POLLARD.

10

HEAVENLY JOY ON EARTH.

Come, we who love the Lord,
  And let our joys be known ;
Join in a song with sweet accord,
  And thus surround the throne.

    We're marching to Zion,
    Beautiful, beautiful Zion,
    We're marching upward to Zion,
    The beautiful city of God.

Let those refuse to sing,
  Who never knew our God!
But fav'rites of the heav'nly King
  Should speak their joys abroad.

    We're marching to Zion, etc.

The men of grace have found
  Glory begun below:
Celestial fruits on earthly ground,
  From faith and hope may grow.

    We're marching to Zion, etc.

The hill of Zion yields
  A thousand sacred sweets,
Before we reach the heav'nly fields
  Or walk the golden streets.

    We're marching to Zion, etc.

Then let our songs abound,
  And every tear be dry ;
We're marching thro' Immanuel's ground,
  To fairer worlds on high.

    We're marching to Zion, etc.

THE LORD IS MY SHEPHERD.

[From the Sabbath School Bell, No. 1, page 68.]

The Lord is my Shepherd; I shall not want.

He maketh me to lie down in green pastures:
He leadeth me beside the still waters.

He restoreth my soul:
He leadeth me in the paths of righteousnes for his
name's sake.

Yea, though I walk through the valley of the shadow
of death, I will fear no evil:
For thou art with me: thy rod and thy staff they
comfort me.

Thou preparest a table before me in the presence of
mine enemies.
Thou anointest my head with oil: my cup runneth
over.

Surely goodness and mercy shall follow me all the days
of my life:
And I will dwell in the house of the Lord forever.

DON'T YOU HEAR THE ANGELS COMING?

[From the Sabbath School Bell, No. 2, page 6.]

Holy angels in their flight,
Traverse over earth and sky,
Acts of kindness their delight,
Winged with mercy as they fly.
Don't you hear them coming over hill and plain
Scattering music in their heavenly train!
Oh! don't you hear the angels coming,
Singing as they come?
Oh! bear me angels,
Angels bear me home.

Tho' their forms we cannot see,
   They attend and guard our way,
Till we join their company
   In the fields of heavenly day.
     Don't you hear, etc.

Had we but an angel's wing,
   And an angel's heart of flame,
Oh, how sweetly would we ring
   Thro' the world the Saviour's name.
     Don't you hear, etc.

Yet methinks if I should die,
   And become an angel too,
I, perhaps, like them might fly,
   And the Saviour's bidding do
     Don't you hear, etc.

THE CHRISTIAN'S MISSION.

[From the Singing Pilgrim, page 91.]

Brother, you may work for Jesus;
   God has given you a place
In some portion of his vineyard,
   And will give sustaining grace.
He has bidden you "Go labor"
   And has promised a reward,
Even joy and life eternal
   In the kingdom of your Lord,
   In the kingdom of your Lord.

Brother, you may pray for Jesus
   In your closet and at home,
In the village in the city,
   Or wherever you may roam;
Pray that God may send the spirit
   Into some dear sinner's heart,
And that in his soul's salvation
   You may bear some humble part,
   You may bear some humble part.

Brother, you may "sing for Jesus;"
  O how precious is his love!
Praise him for his boundless blessings
  Ever coming from above.
Sing how Jesus died to save you,
  How your sin and guilt he bore;
How his blood hath sealed your pardon:
  "Sing for Jesus" evermore,
  "Sing for Jesus" evermore.

Brother, you may live for Jesus,
  Him who died that you might live
O then all your ransomed powers
  Cheerful to his service give.
Thus for Jesus you may labor,
  And for Jesus sing and pray;
Consecrate your life to Jesus —
  Love and serve him every day,
  Love and serve him every day.

NEARER, MY GOD, TO THEE.

[From the Musical Leaves, page 10.]

Nearer, my God, to thee,
  Nearer to thee,
  E'en though it be a cross
That raiseth me,
  Still all my song shall be,
Nearer, my God, to thee,
  Nearer to thee.
Nearer, my God, to thee,

Though like a wanderer,
  Daylight all gone,
Darkness be over me,
  My rest a stone,
Yet in my dreams I'd be
  Nearer, my God, to thee.
    Nearer, my God, etc.

There let the way appear,
　Steps up to heaven;
All that thou sendest me
　In mercy given,
Angels to beckon me,
　Nearer, my God, to thee.
　　Nearer, my God, etc.

Then with my waking thoughts,
　Bright with thy praise,
Out of my stony griefs,
　Bethel I'll raise;
So by my woes to be
　Nearer, my God, to thee.
　　Nearer, my God, etc.

Or, if on joyful wing,
　Cleaving the sky,
Sun, moon, and stars forgot,
　Upward I fly,
Still, all my song shall be,
　Nearer, my God, to thee
　　Nearer, my God, etc.

IF I WERE AN ANGEL.

[From the Dove, page 24.]

If I were an angel, with a bright and starry crown,
　And a harp that rung the sweetest notes of song;
I would stoop in love and pity, I would kindly hasten
　　　down
To the weary ones in sorrow waiting long.

　O, sweet mercy, sweet angel mercy,
　Lovely and gentle as the dawn,
Bending softly o'er the lowly, breathing hope
　　and heav'nly light,　　　　　....
From thy dwelling in the radiant courts of morn.

If I were an angel, with a harp of sweetest song,
    I would hasten on the pinions of the dove;
I would guide the erring children from the paths of
        sin and wrong,
    To the folds of Him whose sweetest name is Love
        O, sweet mercy, etc.

If I were an angel, with a crown of purest gold,
    I would came with flow'rs of mercy for the poor;
I would whisper of the Saviour and the glories all
        untold;
    I would seek to open every prison door.
        O, sweet mercy, etc.

COME FROM THE HILL TOP.

[From the Dove, page 31.]

Come from the hill-top, the vale, and the glen,
Lights now the Sabbath the landscape again;
Little feet patter like rain o'er the sod,
On in the path to the temple of God.

    On to the temple, On to the temple,
    On to the temple, On to the temple,
    Little feet patter like rain on the sod,
    On in the path to the temple of God.

Who to the fields or the forest would stray,
Seeking their pleasure at work or at play?
Who, when that banner of love is unfurl'd,
Turn to the bubble-like joys of the world.
    On to the temple, etc.

We from the service of Sin would depart,
Heeding Thy mandate of "Give me thine heart;"
Suffer the children to "come unto me,"
Saviour, behold at Thy feet here are we.
    On to the temple, etc.

Thus when our Sabbaths on earth are no more,
We shall be with Thee, and love and adore;
Singing in heaven, that bright world of bliss,
Songs that we learn'd on the Sabbaths of this.
    On to the temple, etc.

I'LL NEVER DESPAIR.

[From the Sabbath School Trumpet, page 82.]

Oh God, my heart is faint and weak,
   And wav'ring is my faith;
But thou canst give thy children strength,
   To triumph over death.
      I'll never despair, though the tempests war,
       And the waves of sorrow rise;
      I'll look beyond the storms of earth,
       To my home beyond the skies.

And thou canst give the steadfast faith
   Of holy men of old,
Who did through untold future years,
   The promises behold.
      I'll never despair, etc.

'Tis thine, when all is cold and dead,
   To bid the sinner live,
And Faith, and Hope, and Charity,
   They all are thine to give.
      I'll never despair, etc.

Thy gift, the love as strong as death,
   Which holy martyrs felt,
As calmly by the fun'ral pile,
   With upward glance they knelt.
      I'll never despair, etc.

OUT ON THE OCEAN SAILING.

[From the Golden Censer, page 98.]

We are out on the ocean sailing,
  Homeward bound we sweetly glide;
We are out on the ocean sailing,
  To a home beyond the tide.
      All the storms will soon be over,
        Then we'll anchor in the harbor,
      We are out on the ocean sailing,
        To a home beyond the tide.

Millions now are safely landed
  Over on the golden shore;
Millions more are on their journey,
  Yet there's room for millions more.
      All the storms, etc.

Spread your sails, while heavenly breezes
  Gently waft our vessel on;
All on board are sweetly singing—
  Free salvation is the song.
      All the storms, etc.

When we all are safely anchored,
  We will shout—our trials o'er;
We will walk about the city,
  And we'll sing for evermore.
      All the storms, etc.

THE STAR-SPANGLED BANNER.

[From the Golden Chain, page 22.]

O say, can you see by the dawn's early light,
　What so proudly we hailed at the twilight's last gleaming,
Whose broad stripes and bright stars, thro' the perilous fight,
　O'er the ramparts we watched, were so gallantly streaming.
And the rocket's red glare, bombs bursting in air,
Gave proof thro' the night that our flag was still there:
　　O say does that star-spangled banner yet wave
　　O'er the land of the free and the home of the brave.

On the shore dimly seen thro' the mists of the deep,
　Where the foe's haughty host in dread silence reposes,
What is that which the breeze, o'er the towering steep, .
　As it fitfully blows. half conceals, half discloses;
Now it catches the gleam of the morning's first beam,
In full glory reflected now shines in the stream:
　　'Tis the star-spangled banner, O long may it wave
　　O'er the land of the free and the home of the brave.

And where is that band, who so vauntingly swore,
　That the havoc of war and the battle's confusion,
A home and a country should leave us no more—
　Their blood has washed out their foul footsteps' pollution,
No refuge can save the hireling and slave,
From the terror of flight. or the gloom of the grave:
　　And the star-spangled banner in triumph shall wave
　　O'er the land of the free and the home of the brave.

O thus be it ever, when freemen shall stand
　Between their loved home and the war's desolation;
Blest with victory and peace, may the heaven-rescued land
　Praise the power that hath made and preserved us a nation.
Then conquer we must, when our cause it is just,
And this be our motto—" In GOD is our trust ! "
　　And the star-spangled banner in triumph shall wave
　　O'er the land of the free and the home of the brave.

EVENING SONG.

[From the Fresh Laurels, page 10.]

'Tis sweet to think, as night comes on,
    Dark and drear, dark and drear,
Ere "stars come twinkling, one by one,"
    Earth to cheer, earth to cheer,
        There is a world where comes no night.

'Tis sweet to think when round us lie,
    Grief and care, grief and care,
Our Jesus hears the softest sigh,
    Breath'd in pray'r, breath'd in pray'r,
        And if we love him, we shall see.

It needs no sun or moon to light,
For Jesus' presence makes it bright —
    No night there, no night there.
That "land from sin and sorrow free,"
And, oh! we know that there will be
    No tears there, no tears there.

THE LOVE OF JESUS.

[From the Fresh Laurels, page 10.]

I know 'tis Jesus loves my soul,
And makes the wounded spirit whole;
My nature is by sin defiled,
Yet Jesus loves a little child.

How kind is Jesus, oh, how good,
'Twas for my soul he shed his blood;
For children's sake he was reviled,
For Jesus loves a little child.

When I offend, by thought or tongue,
Omit the right, or do the wrong,
If I repent he's reconciled,
For Jesus loves a little child.

To me may Jesus now impart,
Altho' so young, a gracious heart;
Alas! I'm oft by sin defiled,
Yet Jesus loves a little child.

WANDERER.

[From the Fresh Laurels, page 20.]

Jesus, I come to thee, a wand'rer, a wand'rer,
    A stranger from my Father's house
I would no longer be:
    Jesus, I plead with thee, a wand'rer, a wand'rer,
O wash me in thy cleansing blood,
    And set my spirit free.

CHORUS—

Now blessed Saviour, take thy weary wand'ring child,
Keep me, O keep me from the tempest wild,
My lonely heart by sin oppressed
Would lose its burden on thy breast,
And find a calm and peaceful rest, forever, there.

Jesus, the living way, O save me, O save me;
    O lead me to the precious fold,
And let me never stray:
    O let me hear thy voice, my Father, dear Father,
In gentle tones my pardon speak,
    And bid my soul rejoice.

CHORUS—

Jesus, the way is bright before me, before me,
    My prayer is heard, the clouds are gone,
I see thy glorious light:
    Jesus, no more I'll roam a wand'rer, a wand'rer,
My Father holds me in his arms,
    And bids me welcome home.
CHORUS—

OUR LOST ONE.

[From the Fresh Laurels, page 21.]

There's a quiet valley,
    Sheltered by the hills,
Where the song-birds rally,
    Near the shaded rills,
And the tinted flowers,
    Fairy-like and pure,
From their sylvan bowers
    Balmy zephyrs lure.

Smiling, lovely creature
    Joyous as the day,
Fair of form and feature,
    Happy, blithe and gay,
Music's rippling sweetness,
    Laugh and careless song,
From her heart's repleteness,
    Ever flowed along.

REFRAIN—
There we laid our loved one, our loved one, our loved one,
There we laid our loved one in her mossy bed,
And the dewy lilies, the lilies, the lilies,
And the dewy lilies crown her peaceful head.

Few the starry summers
    O'er her path had shone,
Ere the angels called her
    To the far unknown.

Smiles and gleamy brightness
   Wreathed that fair young face,
Till its placid whiteness
   Told of death's embrace.

REFRAIN—

THE LAND OF EDEN.

[From the Fresh Laurels, page 22.]

O Eden land, thou land of bloom,
Beyond the shadows of the tomb,
Beyond the pain, and grief, and strife,
That dim and mar our mortal life.
O Eden land, thou land of the blest,
Where we alone find peace and rest.
    O Eden land, thou land of the blest,
    Where we alone find peace and rest.

O Eden land — bright world of bliss,
More fresh and fair, and pure than this;
O! how our weary spirits long
To reach that clime of light and song!
Thou Eden land, at whose close gate
The treasures of our future wait.

    O Eden land, etc.

Thou Eden land, O! could we grasp
Thy promised blessings in our clasp,
Fain would we loose our hold on earth,
And rise to that immortal birth,
Which shall alone place in our hand
The key to Heaven's fair Eden land.

    O Eden land, etc.

LOVE FOR JESUS.

[From the Fresh Laurels, page 23.]

I love the name of Jesus,
That name the angels sing:
And with their loud hosannas,
The heavenly portals ring.
To him my all confiding,
In him my joy complete,
I learn, with Christian meekness,
My duty at his feet.

CHORUS—

I love, I love, I love the name of Jesus,
The sweetest name, the name,
The name the angels sing.
I love, I love, the sweetest name,
The name the angels sing.

I love to think of Jesus,
When all is calm and still;
When pure and holy feelings,
My grateful bosom fill.
I love to think of Jesus,
Whose mercy crowns my days,
How just are all his counsels,
And true are all his ways.

CHORUS—

I love to work for Jesus,
And worship at his throne;
O, may his spirit help me
To live for him alone.
To labor for my Saviour,
My greatest joy shall be;
I know that Jesus loves me,
Because he died for me.

CHORUS—

SUNDAY SCHOOL VOLUNTEER SONG.

[From the Fresh Laurels, page 30.]

We are marching on with shield and banner bright,
We will work for God and battle for the right,
We will praise his name, rejoicing in his might,
    And we'll work till Jesus calls.
In the Sunday School our army we prepare,
As we rally round our blessed standard there,
And the Saviour's cross we early learn to bear,
    While we work till Jesus calls.

CHORUS—

    We are marching onward, singing as we go,
    To the promised land where living waters flow;
    Come and join our ranks as pilgrims here below,
      Come and work till Jesus calls.
Then awake, then awake, happy song, happy song,
Shout for joy, shout for joy, as we gladly march along.
Then awake, then awake, happy song, happy song,
Shout for joy, shout for joy, as we gladly march along.

We are marching on, our Captain, ever near,
Will protect us still, his gentle voice we hear;
Let the foe advance, we'll never, never fear,
    For we'll work till Jesus calls.
Then awake, awake, our happy, happy song,
We will shout for joy, and gladly march along;
In the Lord of Hosts let every heart be strong,
    While we work till Jesus calls.

CHORUS—

We are marching on the straight and narrow way,
That will lead to life and everlasting day,
To the smiling fields that never will decay,
   But we'll work till Jesus calls.
We are marching on and pressing toward the prize,
To a glorious crown beyond the glowing skies,
To the radiant fields where pleasure never dies,
   And we'll work till Jesus calls.

CHORUS—

JESUS, DEAR, I COME TO THEE.

[From the Fresh Laurels, page 31.]

Jesus, dear, I come to thee,
   Thou hast said I may;
Tell me what my life should be,
   Take my sins away.
Jesus, dear, I learn of thee,
   In thy word divine,
Every promise there I see,
   May I call it mine.

CHORUS—Jesus hear my humble song,
     I am weak, but thou art strong,
     Gently lead my soul along,
     Help me come to thee.

Jesus, dear, I long for thee,
   Long thy peace to know,
Grant those purer joys to me,
   Earth can ne'er bestow;
Jesus, dear, I cling to thee;
   When my heart is sad,
Thou wilt kindly speak to me,
   Thou wilt make me glad.

CHORUS—Jesus, hear, etc.

11

Jesus, dear, I trust in thee,
  Trust thy tender love,
There's a happy home for me,
  With thy saints above;
Jesus, I would come to thee,
  Thou hast said I may,
Tell me what my life should be,
  Take my sins away.

RIGHT AWAY.

[From the Fresh Laurels, page 33.]

I will come to Jesus right away, right away,
'Tis his Spirit calls me, I obey;
      Jesus will receive me,
      He will never leave me,
I will come to Jesus right away, right away.
      I will come to Jesus right away.

I will pray to Jesus right away, right away,
I will seek his blessing every day;
      While my heart is pleading,
      He is interceding,
I will pray to Jesus right away.
      I will pray to Jesus right away.

I will live for Jesus right away, right away,
'Tis my Saviour calls me, I obey;
      Now in childhood's morning
      Is the gentle warning,
I will live for Jesus right away.
      I will live for Jesus right away.

I will work for Jesus right away, right away,
Labor in his vineyard every day;
      With my heart pursuing
      What my hands are doing,
  I will work for Jesus every day.
      I will work for Jesus every day.

PRAYER FOR GUIDANCE.

[From the Fresh Laurels, page 42.]

Jesus lead me, Jesus guide me,
  In the way I ought to go;
Help an erring one to praise thee,
  Teach me, Lord, thy word to know.
Tho' my heart is weak and sinful,
  May I bring it, Lord, to thee;
Wash me in thy precious fountain;
  Jesus, thou hast died for me.

In thy word I read the promise —
  Ask for mercy and receive;
They who early seek shall find me:
  Lord, I will, I do believe.
Jesus hear me, Jesus guide me,
  In the way that leads to thee,
Blessed hope, my only comfort,
  Jesus, thou hast died for me.

Happy now, my soul has found thee,
  I can sing thy praise divine;
I can tell the world around me,
  I am thine, forever thine.
Thou wilt lead me, thou wilt guide me,
  Sweetly now I rest on thee;
Blessed hope, my only comfort,
  Jesus, thou hast died for me.

SWEET THE SABBATH MORNING.

[From the Fresh Laurels, page 47.]

Sweet the Sabbath morning, calm and bright returning,
  Seems to subdue the turmoil of the week;
Every Sabbath morning, see their footsteps turning,
  Where they learn to sing and speak a Saviour's praise.
Sabbath bells inviting, children all uniting,
  Sweetly sing the praise of him whose throne they seek ;
Jesus is near them, Jesus will hear them,
  Yes, he will hear those sweet notes they raise.

Sweetest day of seven! pointing us to heaven;
  Thou beacon-light upon life's stormy sea!
Rest we from our labor, sharing with our neighbor,
  All the holy peace and joy that comes with thee.
Sweet Sabbath morning, blest thy returning,
  Oh! may we treasure the Sabbath days.
Hark! a voice is calling, through the stillness falling,
  Calling us to meet and sing our Saviour's praise.

Every Sabbath morning, sinful pleasure scorning,
  Our Sunday-school shall be a sacred spot:
There our voices ringing, with the angels singing,
  Lead our thoughts away where care and sin are not.
Oh, holy pleasure! Oh, heavenly treasure!
  We'll ever prize these sweet Sabbath days!
Bringing heaven nearer; making Jesus dearer;
  Fitting us to join his saints, and see his face.

NEARER THE KINGDOM.

[From the Fresh Laurels, page 49.]

Blessed Redeemer, how precious thou art,
    Full of compassion and grace;
Sweet is the music of joy to my heart,
    Cheered by the smile of thy face.

      CHORUS—Nearer the kingdom of glory to-day,
            Nearer, my Father, to thee,
            Upward my spirit is soaring away,
            Pleasure immortal I see.

Shadows of darkness no longer I fear,
    Jesus, I know thou art mine;
Hark! 'tis the anthem of rapture I hear,
    Wafted from regions divine.

    CHORUS — Nearer the kingdom, etc.

Onward, still onward, my refuge and guide,
    Gladly my way I pursue;
Bright is my path while I walk by thy side,
    Thou wilt my courage renew.

    CHORUS — Nearer the kingdom, etc.

Nearer the fount where my soul shall be free,
    Nearer the angels above;
Nearer the crown thou hast purchased for me,
    Jeweled with mercy and love.

    CHORUS — Nearer the kingdom, etc.

THE WATER OF LIFE.

[From the Fresh Laurels, page 50.]

Jesus, the water of life will give
    Freely, freely, freely.
Jesus, the water of life will give
    Freely to those who love him.
Come to that fountain, O drink and live,
    Freely freely, freely,
Come to that fountain, O drink and live,
    Flowing for those that love him.

CHORUS—The Spirit and the bride say, come
        Freely, freely, freely,
. . And he that is thirsty let him come
        And drink of the water of life.
    The fountain of life is flowing,
        Flowing, freely flowing,
    The fountain of life is flowing,
        Is flowing for you and for me.

Jesus has promised a home in heaven,
    Freely, freely, freely,
Jesus has promised a home in heaven,
    Freely to those that love him.
Treasures unfading will there be given,
    Freely, freely, freely,
Treasures unfading will there be given,
    Freely to those that love him.

CHORUS — The Spirit and the bride say come, etc.

Jesus has promised a robe of white,
 Freely, freely, freely,
Jesus has promised a robe of white,
 Freely to those that love him;
Kingdoms of glory and crowns of light,
 Freely, freely, freely,
Kingdoms of glory and crowns of light,
 Freely to those that love him.

Chorus — The Spirit and the bride say, come, etc.

Jesus has promised eternal day,
 Freely, freely, freely,
Jesus has promised eternal day,
 Freely to those that love him;
Pleasure that never shall pass away,
 Freely, freely, freely,
Pleasure that never shall pass away,
 Freely to those that love him.

Chorus — The Spirit and the bride say, come, etc.

Jesus has promised a calm repose,
 Freely, freely, freely,
Jesus has promised a calm repose,
 Freely to all that love him;
Come to the water of life that flows,
 Freely, freely, freely,
Come to the water of life that flows,
 Freely to all that love him.

Chorus — The Spirit and the bride say, come, etc.

NEVER GROW WEARY.

[From the Fresh Laurels, page 60.]

We must never grow weary, doing well, doing well,
    Though in time we may reap no reward;
For eternity will tell — yes, eternity will tell,
    What a blessing rests on those who serve the Lord.

CHORUS — O ye stars! shine on, shine on!
           Far up in heaven's own blue,
           Some time, some time, I, too, may shine,
           I may shine as brightly as you!

We must bear the yoke daily: — Jesus says,
    "It is easy, my burden is light;"
For he knows how frail we are, yes, he knows how
    frail we are,
    And he helps us through the day and through the
    night.
CHORUS — O ye stars! shine on, etc.

All the stars o'er us shining in the sky,
    And the sun and the moon do his will;
And we know that by and by, if to serve him well
    we try.
    With a brighter glow our spirits he will fill.
CHORUS — O ye stars! shine on, etc.

We must ever be watchful! — for to-day
    May, for you, and for me, be the last;
So the work we'll not delay, but we'll labor, and we'll
    pray,
    Till the sunset hour of life is safely passed.
CHORUS — O ye stars! shine on, etc.

WHO SHALL SHINE?

[From the Fresh Laurels, page 62.]

The beauteous stars that shine
  So bright in yonder sky,
Like jewels fitly set,
  Whose lustre cannot die;
And may I ever hope,
  Their wondrous height t' obtain,
And see the glory they beheld
  On old Judea's plain?

CHORUS — They that are wise shall shine,
    They shall shine as bright as the stars,
    They shall shine as bright as the stars
    That shine upon us from on high.
    They shall shine as bright as the stars,
      As the stars that shine upon us from on
        high.

Oh, to be truly wise,
  In thought, in word, in deed;
To teach my erring heart,
  To seek the help I need!
Thou ruler of the world,
  Who keep'st the stars in place,
Oh, grant that I may yet behold
  The brightness of thy face.

CHORUS — They that are wise shall shine, etc.

If wisdom's ways I seek,
  I surely shall be blest;
They run through joy and peace,
  Unto a land of rest;

And oh, I fain would reach
Those starry heights above.
And with new brightness ever shine,
And sing a Saviour's love.

CHORUS — They that are wise shall shine, etc.

AWAY! AWAY!

[From the Fresh Laurels, page 72.]

Away! away! not a moment to linger,
Haste we now with footstep free,
Where those who love in the vineyard to labor,
Wait for you and me.

CHORUS—To the Sunday-school rejoicing we will go,
'Tis a place where all are happy here below,
Where the way of life we learn to know,
And seek our home above.

Away! away! where the angels are bending
Lightly o'er the house of prayer,
Glad hymns of praise to the Lord of the Sabbath,
Sweetly echo there.

CHORUS—To the Sunday-school rejoicing we will go, etc.

Away! away! for the moments are flying,
Time for us will soon be o'er;
This holy day we will try to improve it,
Ere its light is o'er.

CHORUS—To the Sunday-school rejoicing we will go, etc.

Away! away! not a moment to linger,
Haste we now with footstep free,
Where those who love in the vineyard to labor
Wait for you and me.

CHORUS—To the Sunday-school rejoicing we will go, etc.

MIGHTY TO SAVE.

[From the Fresh Laurels, page 82.]

There is light in the valley once shrouded with darkness,
  Hope sheds her bright ray o'er the gloom of the grave,
A Saviour, ascending, fills earth with his brightness,
  'Tis Jesus, 'tis Jesus, the mighty to save.

CHORUS — Mighty to save, mighty to save,
      'Tis Jesus, 'tis Jesus, the mighty to save.

O'er the dark realms of death, shines a halo of glory,
  The tyrant no longer exerts his dread sway;
His dark reign is ended, his scepter is broken,
  Henceforth all his subjects, his subjects are free.

CHORUS — Mighty to save, etc.

Shout aloud, ye redeemed ones, repeat the glad story,
  And sing, all ye ransomed from death's dismal thrall;
In triumph ascend to the mansions of glory,
  Forever, forever restored from the fall.

CHORUS — Mighty to save, etc.

There, O there, on the banks of the beautifulriver,
  Shall anthems of rapture unceasingly rise;
While angels and saints, reunited forever,
  Unite in the chorus that gladdens the skies.

CHORUS — Mighty to save, etc.

IN A MANGER LAID SO LOWLY.

[From the Fresh Laurels, page 84.]

In a manger laid so lowly,
    Came the Prince of Peace to earth;
While a choir of angels holy,
    Sang to celebrate his birth.
      "Glory in the highest,"
      Sang the glad angelic strain;
      "Glory in the highest,"
"Peace on earth, good will to men,"
"Peace on earth, good will to men."

As the wise men from far Persia
    Brought rich gifts to Jewry's King,
Grateful love, a richer treasure,
    Would we as our offering bring.
      "Glory in the highest,"
      Let us join th' angelic strain;
      "Glory in the highest,"
"Peace on earth, good will to men,"
"Peace on earth, good will to men."

Where Christ's joyful kingdom cometh,
    Deserts blossom as the rose;
And God's gracious rain descendeth,
    Where the coral island grows.
      "Glory in the highest,"
      Once more sing th' angelic strain;
      "Glory in the highest,"
"Peace on earth, good will to men,"
"Peace on earth, good will to men."

MY HOME IS THERE.

[From the Fresh Laurels, page 94.]

Above the waves of earthly strife,
Above the ills and cares of life,
Where all is peaceful, bright, and fair;
My home is there, my home is there.

CHORUS —

My beautiful home, my beautiful home,
In the land where the glorified ever shall roam,
Where angels bright wear crowns of light,
My home is there, my home is there.
My beautiful, beautiful home,
My beautiful home, in the land where the glorified
ever shall roam,
Where angels, angels bright, wear crowns, wear
crowns of light,
My home is there, my home is there.

Where living fountains sweetly flow,
Where buds and flowers immortal grow
Where trees their fruits celestial bear;
My home is there, my home is there.

CHOURS — My beautiful home, etc.

Away from sorrow, doubt and pain,
Away from worldly loss and gain,
From all temptation, tears and care;
My home is there, my home is there.

CHORUS — My beautiful home, etc.

Beyond the bright and pearly gates,
Where Jesus, loving Saviour, waits,
Where all is peaceful, bright and fair;
My home is there, my home is there.

CHORUS — My beautiful home etc.

WILL THE ANGELS COME TO ME?

[From the Fresh Laurels, page 114.]

Oh, I see the shining angels,
Gath'ring round my dying bed,
With their harps and crown of glory;
Thus a faithful mother said,
While celestial songs were ringing
Thro' the heavenly courts above,
Seraphs from glory bringing
Blessed words of peace and love.

CHORUS — When I near death's stormy billow,
And earth's scenes no more can see,
When I press my dying pillow,
Will the angels come to me?
Will they come, will they come,
Will the angels come to me,
Will they come, will they come?
Will they come,
Will the angels come to me?
Will they come, will they come,
Will they come, will they come,
Will they come?

Earthly joys, I know, are fleeting;
Earthly pleasures quickly go;
But the joys that last forever,
From the heavenly fountain flow!

When released from life's short duty,
  My glad spirit would be free:—
From that land of peace and beauty,
  Will the angels come to me?

CHORUS — When I near death's stormy billow, etc.

Oh, how sweet to feel their presence,
  In the hushed and silent room;
With their bright and shining faces,
  Gilding all the dreaded gloom!
When from loved friends I've parted,
  And their tears are flowing free;
When from Jordan's banks I've started,
  Will the angels come to me?

CHORUS — When I near death's stormy billow, etc.

GOING HOME.

[From the Little Sunbeam, page 24.]

We're going to a happy home,
  Going home. going home;
To join with those before us gone,
  Going home, going home.
To clasp again in fond embrace,
  The loved ones of that happy place,
And see our Saviour face to face,
  Going home, going home.

CHORUS — Going home, going home,
      Yes, we're going home;
    We'll gladly shout when death draws near,
      We're going, going home.

O! peaceful is that blessed shore,
  Going home. going home;
Where ills of life afflict no more,
  Going home, going home.

The sorrowing pilgrim finds release,
  The weary rest in perfect peace,
And pain and death forever cease,
  Going home, going home.

CHORUS — Going home, going home, etc.

We are going, O, what joys arise!
  Going home, going home,
Hopes of that blissful paradise,
  Going home, going home.
Then let our feeble bodies die,
  We have a mansion in the sky,
We'll gladly shout when death is nigh,
  Going home, going home.

CHORUS — Going home, going ome, etc.

"WAITING, ONLY WAITING."

[From the Little Sunbeam, page 50.]

Only waiting till the shadows
  Are a little longer grown,
Only waiting till the glimmer
  Of the day's last beam is flown.
Till the night of earth is faded
  From the heart once full of day —
Till the stars of heaven are breaking,
  Thro' the twilight soft and gray.

CHORUS — Waiting, waiting, waiting till the shadows
  Waiting, waiting. waiting till the shadows,
    Are a little longer grown.

Only waiting till the reapers
  Have the last sheaf gathered home;
For the summer time is faded,
  And the autumn winds have come

Quickly, reapers, quickly gather,
　　The last ripe hours of my heart,
For the bloom of life is withered,
　　And I hasten to depart.

CHORUS — Waiting, waiting, etc.

Only waiting till the angels,
　　Open wide the mystic gate,
At whose feet I long have lingered,
　　Weary, poor and desolate.
Even now I hear their footsteps,
　　And their voices far away,
If they call me I am waiting,
　　Only waiting to obey.

CHORUS — Waiting, waiting, etc.

Only waiting till the shadows
　　Are a little longer grown,
Only waiting till the glimmer
　　Of the day's last beam is done;
Then, from out the gathering darkness,
　　Holy, deathless stars arise,
By whose light my soul shall gladly
　　Tread its pathway to the skies.

CHORUS — Waiting, waiting, etc.

PLEA FOR MERCY.

[From the Singing Pilgrim, page 14.]

Depth of mercy can there be,
Mercy still reserved for me?
Can my God his wrath forbear,
Me, the chief of sinners, spare?

12

CHORUS—God is love, I know, I feel;
Jesus weeps and loves me still;
Jesus weeps, he weeps and loves me still.

I have long withstood his grace,
Long provoked him to his face;
Would not hearken to his calls;
Grieved him by a thousand falls.

CHORUS—God is love, etc.

Now incline me to repent;
Let me now my sins lament,
Now my foul revolt deplore,
Weep, believe, and sin no more.

CHORUS—God is love, etc.

There for me the Saviour stands,
Shows his wounds, and spreads his hands;
God is love, I know, I feel;
Jesus weeps, and loves me still.

CHORUS—God is love, etc.

ZEPHYR.

[From the Golden Censer, page 11.]

Soft be the gently breathing notes,
That sing the Saviour's dying love;
Soft as the evening zephyr floats,
And soft as tuneful lyres above.

Soft as the morning dews descend,
While warbling birds exulting soar;
So soft to our almighty Friend
Be every sigh our bosoms pour.

Pure as the sun's enlivening ray,
  That scatters life and joy abroad;
Pure as the lucid orb of day,
  That wide proclaims its Maker, God.

THE CROSS OF CHRIST.

[From the Golden Censer, page 21.]

In the cross of Christ I glory,
  Towering o'er the wrecks of time;
All the light of sacred story
  Gathers round its head sublime.

When the woes of life o'ertake me,
  Hopes deceive and fears annoy,
Never shall the cross forsake me;
  Lo! it glows with peace and joy.

When the sun of bliss is beaming
  Light and love upon my way,
From the cross the radiance streaming
  Adds new luster to the day.

Bane and blessing, pain and pleasure,
  By the cross are sanctified;
Peace is there that knows no measure,
  Joys that through all time abide.

In the cross of Christ I glory,
  Towering o'er the wrecks of time;
All the lights of sacred story
  Gathers round its head sublime.

CHILDREN'S PRAISES.

[From the Golden Censer, page 16.]

When Hosannas loud resounding
  Rang through Salem joyfully,
As the Saviour came in triumph,
  Children's voices rose on high,
Hymning out the joyful chorus,
  Shouting forth the glad acclaim,
"Mighty King, the son of David,
  Coming in Jehovah's name."

Jesus heard their little voices,
  And with gentle, loving face,
Smiled upon the happy children
  Subjects of his royal grace;
Hushed the haughty priests to silence
  By the old prophetic word:
" Forth from infant lips perfected,
  Praise shall come before the Lord."

Still the mighty King of Salem
  Comes in holy triumph nigh,
Still hosannas, loud resounding,
  Rise from infant tongues on high,
Still the skeptic and the scoffer
  Sneer and ridicule the song,
And the Saviour smiles as sweetly
  On the happy infant throng.

In the day when gathered millions
  Sing hosannas, far away,
'Mid the shining hosts of angels,
  Infant tongues shall swell the lay.
Come then, children, to the Saviour,
  Sweetest welcome waits you here;
And with those bright hosts in heaven,
  You shall sing his praises there.

"PRECIOUS IS THE TIME."

[From the Golden Censer, page 45.]

We must labor while 'tis day,
  Precious is the time;
Soon the light will fade away,
  Precious is the time;
Whatsoe'er we find to do,
Let us with our might pursue,
Keeping still one thought in view,
  Precious is the time.
      Precious is the time, friends!
      Precious is the time, friends!
      We must labor while 'tis day,
      Precious is the time.

Do we try the right to choose,
  Precious is the time;
Not a moment should we lose,
  Precious is the time;
Life is like a morning flower,
Blooming in a fragrant bower,
Drooping, dying in an hour,
  Precious is the time.
      Precious is the time, etc.

Have we sought our Father's love?
  Precious is the time;
Live we for our home above?
  Precious is the time;
Do we daily kneel in prayer,
Thanking God for all his care,
Grateful for the gifts we share?
  Precious is the time.
      Precious is the time, etc.

We must labor while 'tis day,
Precious is the time;
Soon the light will fade away,
Precious is the time;
Whatsoe'er we find to do,
Let us with our might pursue,
Keeping still one thought in view,
Precious is the time.
Precious is the time, etc.

GO AND TELL JESUS.

[From the Golden Censer, page 61.]

Go and tell Jesus, weary, sin-sick soul,
He'll ease thee of thy burden, make thee whole;
Look up to him, he only can forgive,
Believe on him and thou shalt surely live.
Go and tell Jesus,
He only can forgive,
Go and tell Jesus,
O turn to him and live.
Go and tell Jesus,
Go and tell Jesus,
Go and tell Jesus,
He only can forgive.

Go and tell Jesus, when your sins arise
Like mountains of deep guilt before your eyes:
His blood was spilt, his precious life he gave,
That mercy, peace and pardon you might have.
Go and tell Jesus, etc.

Go and tell Jesus, he'll dispel thy fears,
Will calm thy doubts, and wipe away thy tears;
He'll take thee in his arm, and on his breast
Thou mayst be happy, and forever rest.
Go and tell Jesus, etc.

JESUS' LITTLE LAMB.

[From the Golden Censer, page 43.]

I am Jesus' little Lamb,
Therefore glad and gay I am;
Jesus loves me, Jesus knows me,
All that's good and fair he shows me,
Tends me every day the same,
Even calls me by my name.

Out and in I safely go,
Want or hunger never know;
Soft green pastures he discloseth,
Where his happy flock reposeth;
When I faint or thirsty be,
To the brook he leadeth me.

Should not I be glad and gay?
In this blessed fold all day;
By this Holy Shepherd tended,
Whose kind arms, when life is ended,
Bear me to the world of light?
Yes! oh, yes, my lot is bright!

SLEEPING IN JESUS.

[From the Golden Censer, page 11.]

Asleep in Jesus! blessed sleep,
From which none ever wakes to weep;
A calm and undisturbed repose,
Unbroken by the last of foes.

Asleep in Jesus! oh, how sweet,
To be for such a slumber meet!
With holy confidence to sing
That death has lost its cruel sting.

Asleep in Jesus! peaceful rest,
Whose waking is supremely blest;
No fear, no woe, shall dim the hour
That manifests the Saviour's power.

Asleep in Jesus! oh, for me
May such a blissful refuge be;
Securely shall my ashes lie,
Waiting a summons from on high.

THANKSGIVING ANTHEM.

[From the Golden Censer, page 64.]

Let every heart rejoice and sing;
  Let choral anthems rise;
Ye reverend men and children bring
  To God your sacrifice.
    For He is good; the Lord is good,
      And kind are all his ways;
    With songs and honors sounding loud,
      The Lord Jehovah praise:
    While the rocks and the rills,
      While the vales and the hills,
    A glorious anthem raise.
Let each prolong the grateful song,
  And the God of our fathers praise,
Let each prolong the grateful song,
  And the God of our fathers praise.

He bids the sun to rise and set;
  In heav'n his power is known;
And earth, subdued to him, shall yet
  Bow low before his throne.
    For he is good; the Lord is good, etc.

JESUS IS MINE.

[From the Golden Censer, page 89.]

Fade, fade each earthly joy,
  Jesus is mine ;
Break every tender tie,
  Jesus is mine ;
Dark is the wilderness,
Earth has no resting place,
Jesus alone can bless,
  Jesus is mine.

Tempt not my soul away,
  Jesus is mine ;
Here would I ever stay,
  Jesus is mine ;
Perishing things of clay,
Born but for one brief day,
Pass from my heart away,
  Jesus is mine.

Farewell, ye dreams of night,
  Jesus is mine ;
Lost in this dawning light,
  Jesus is mine ;
All that my soul has tried,
Left but a dismal void,—
Jesus has satisfied,
  Jesus is mine.

Farewell mortality,
  Jesus is mine ;
Welcome eternity,
  Jesus is mine ;
Welcome, O loved and blest,
Welcome sweet scenes of rest,
Welcome my Saviour's breast,
  Jesus is mine.

A BRIGHT AND GLORIOUS KINGDOM.

[From the Golden Censer, page 90.]

There is a glorious kingdom.
A kingdom bright and fair,
And many little children
Wait on the good King there.
Yes, children, children
Are in that glorious kingdom,
That kingdom, that kingdom,
That kingdom bright and fair.

O, in that glorious kingdom
Is built a throne of gold;
Its ornaments are jewels,
With riches all untold.
A kingdom, kingdom,
A bright and glorious kingdom,
A kingdom, a kingdom,
A kingdom bright and fair.

O, in that glorious kingdom,
And on that golden throne,
There reigns the blessed Saviour,
Those children are his own.
Yes, children, children,
Are in that glorious kingdom;
That kingdom, that kingdom,
That kingdom bright and fair.

And in that glorious kingdom,
Around the throne of gold,
Are throngs of children's angels,
Their numbers are untold.
Yes, angels, angels
Are in that glorious kingdom;
That kingdom, that kingdom,
That kingdom bright and fair.

The children of that kingdom,
  Around that glorious throne,
Have palms and crowns of victory,
  And harps of sweetest tone.
    All singing, singing,
      There in that glorious kingdom;
    That kingdom, that kingdom,
      That kingdom bright and fair.

And now they lift their voices
  In praises loud and sweet,
And cast their crowns of victory
  Down at their Saviour's feet.
    Of victory, victory,
      Their crowns, their crowns of victory;
    Of victory, of victory,
      Their crowns at Jesus' feet.

Come, all who love that kingdom,
  That kingdom bright and fair;
Come, give your hearts to Jesus,
  And dwell forever there.
    And praise him, praise him
      Forever in that kingdom;
    That kingdom, that kingdom,
      That kingdom bright and fair.

DEATH OF A SCHOLAR.

[From the Golden Censer, page 102.]

Sister, thou wast mild and lovely,
  Gentle as the summer breeze;
Pleasant as the air of evening,
  When it floats among the trees.

Peaceful be thy silent slumber,
　Peaceful in the grave so low ;
Thou no more wilt join our number,
　. Thou no more our songs shalt know.

Dearest sister, thou hast left us,
　Here thy loss we deeply feel ;
But 'tis God that hast bereft us ;
　He can still our sorrow heal.

Yet again we hope to meet thee,
　When the day of life is fled ;
Then, in heaven with joy to greet thee,
　Where no farewell tear is shed.

THE CHILDREN'S JUBILEE.

[From the Sunday School Banner, page 100.]

Hosanna, hosanna, hosanna !
　Hosanna be the children's song.
To Christ the children's King,
　His praise to whom our souls belong,
Let all the children sing.
　Hosanna then our songs shall be,
　Hosanna to our King,
　This is the children's jubilee,
　Let all the children sing.
　This is the children's jubilee, jubilee, jubilee,
　This is the children's jubilee,
　Let all the children sing.

Hosanna here in joyful bands,
　Teachers, and taught, proclaim,
And hail with voices, hearts, and hands,
　Our loving Saviour's name.
　　Hosanna, etc.

Hosanna on the wings of night,
  O'er earth and ocean fly,
Till morn to eve, and noon to night,
  And heaven to earth reply.
    Hosanna, etc.

Hosanna, sound from church and hall,
  Let every voice ascend.
And this my watchword, one and all,
  Hosanna, praise the Lord.
    Hosanna, etc.

JOY AT THE CROSS.

[From the Sunday School Banner, page 39.]

Sweet the moments, rich in blessing,
  Which before the cross I spend ;
Life, and health, and peace possessing,
  From the sinner's dying friend.

Love and grief, my heart dividing,
  With my tears his feet I'll bathe ;
Constant still, in faith abiding,
  Life deriving from his death.

Truly blessed is this station,
  Low before his cross to lie ;
While I see divine compassion
  Beaming in his gracious eye.

Here I'll sit, forever viewing
  Mercy streaming in his blood ;
Precious drops my soul bedewing,
  Plead, and claim my peace with God.

BRING IN THE LAMBS.

[From the Golden Censer, page 86.]

Welcome kind friends and teachers dear,
Ye who have toiled from year to year,
To lead us up the heavenly way,
And teach us how to watch and pray.
 Bring in the lambs, the tender lambs,
  O bring them, bring them in to Jesus' fold.
 Bring in the lambs, the tender lambs,
  O bring them, bring them in to Jesus' fold.

" Soon ye shall reap if ye faint not ;"
(O, let that truth be ne'er forgot ;)
" Wait on the Lord,"—" your strength renew,"
" Be zealous," and be hopeful, too.
 Bring in the lambs, the tender lambs, etc.

Bring in the lambs, while yet ye may
Ere Satan claims them for his prey :
So " ye shall shine as stars of light,"
In yonder heaven so fair and bright.
 Bring in the lambs, the tender lambs, etc.

High, high the heavenly rapture burns,
Whene'er a prodigal returns !
Strive, strive that rapture to prolong,
Till earth shall echo back the song.
 Bring in the lambs, the tender lambs, etc.

OLD HUNDRED.

[From the New Golden Chain, page 101.]

Be thou, O God, exalted high,
 And as thy glory fills the sky,
So let it be on earth displayed,
 Till thou art here as there obeyed.

ZION'S PILGRIM.

[From the New Golden Chain, page 26.]

Pilgrims we are to Canaan bound,
  Our journey lies along this road;
This wilderness we travel round,
  To reach the city of our God.
    O happy pilgrims, spotless fair,
    What makes your robes so white appear?
    Our robes are washed in Jesus' blood,
    And we are traveling home to God.

A few more days, or weeks, or years,
  In this dark desert to complain;
A few more sighs, a few more tears,
  And we shall bid adieu to pain.
    O happy pilgrims, etc.

O blessed land! O happy land!
  When shall we reach thy golden shore,
And one redeemed, unbroken band,
  United be forever more?
    O happy pilgrims, etc.

And if our robes are pure and white,
  May we all reach that blessed abode?
O yes, they all shall dwell in light,
  Whose robes are washed in Jesus' blood.
    O happy pilgrims, etc.

We all shall reach that golden shore,
  If here we watch, and fight, and pray;
Strait is the way, and strait the door,
  And none but pilgrims find the way.
    O happy pilgrims, etc.

O, may we meet at last above,
  Amid the holy blood-washed throng,
And sing forever Jesus' love,
  While saints and angels join the song.
    O happy pilgrims, etc.

CHRIST ALL IN ALL.

[From the New Golden Chain, page 73.]

Jesus, I my cross have taken,
  All to leave and follow thee;
Naked, poor, despised, forsaken,
  Thou from hence my all shalt be;
Perish every fond ambition—
  All I've sought, or hoped, or known,
Yet how rich is my condition,—
  God and heaven are still my own.

Let the world despise and leave me,
  They have left my Saviour, too:
Human hearts and looks deceive me:
  Thou art not, like them, untrue.
Oh! while thou dost smile upon me,
  God of wisdom, love and might!
Foes may hate, and friends disown me;
  Show thy face, and all is bright.

Perish, earthly fame and treasure:
  Come disaster, scorn and pain;
In thy service pain is pleasure,
  With thy favor life is gain:
Oh! 'tis not in grief to harm me,
  While thy love is left to me;
Oh! 'twere not in joy to charm me—
  Were that joy unmixed with thee.

OF SUCH IS THE KINGDOM.

[From Happy Voices, page 65.]

Round the throne in glory
  Happy children throng,
And redemption's story
  Wakes the harp and song.
On the verdant mountain,
  By the shining stream,
Or the living fountain,
  Jesus is their theme.
    Glory to the Lamb,
    Praise him and adore;
    Glory to the Lamb
    Forever more.

Robes of snowy whiteness,
  Beautiful and rare;
Crowns of radiant brightness,
  Such those children wear:
Safe from death's bereavement,
  Sorrow and the grave,
Free from sin's enslavement,
  Vict'ry's palm they wave.
    Glory to the Lamb, etc.

Now the skillful fingers
  Sweep the golden lyre;
Not a harper lingers
  In that ransomed choir;
Voices sweetly blending
  With the tuneful string,
To the throne ascending,
  Praise the heavenly King.
    Glory to the Lamb, etc.

13

Children now sojourning
  In a world of sin,
From your follies turning,
  Strive to enter in:
Let your young affections
  Round the Saviour twine;
And 'mid heaven's attractions
  You shall sing and shine.
    Glory to the Lamb, etc.

JERUSALEM ABOVE.

[From Happy Voices, page 157.]

Jerusalem, my happy home,
  Name ever dear to me,
When shall my labors have an end
  In joy and peace and thee?

When shall these eyes thy heaven-built walls
  And pearly gates behold?
Thy bulwarks with salvation strong,
  And streets of shining gold?

Oh, when, thou city of my God,
  Shall I thy courts ascend,
Where congregations ne'er break up,
  And Sabbaths have no end?

There happier bowers than Eden bloom,
  Nor sin, nor sorrow know:
Blest seats, through rude and stormy scenes
  I onward press to you.

Jerusalem, my happy home,
  My soul still pants for thee;
Then shall my labors have an end
  When I thy joys shall see.

THE MERCY-SEAT.

[From the Golden Shower, page 10.]

From ev'ry stormy wind that blows,
From ev'ry swelling tide of woes,
There is a calm, a sure retreat,
'Tis found beneath the Mercy-seat.
The Mercy-seat, the Mercy-seat,
The blessed Mercy-seat.
The Mercy-seat, the Mercy-seat,
The blessed Mercy-seat.

There is a place where Jesus sheds
The oil of gladness on our heads;
A place than all besides more sweet,
It is the blood-bought Mercy-seat.
The Mercy-seat, etc.

There is a scene where spirits blend,
Where friend holds fellowship with friend,
Tho' sundered far, by faith they meet
Around one common Mercy-seat.
The Mercy-seat, etc.

There—there on eagle wings we soar,
And sin and sense seem all no more,
And heaven comes down our souls to greet.
And glory crowns the Mercy-seat.
The Mercy-seat, etc.

THE HOPE OF HEAVEN.

[From Happy Voices, page 155.]

When I can read my title clear
To mansions in the skies,
I bid farewell to every fear,
And wipe my weeping eyes.

Should earth against my soul engage,
And hellish darts be hurled,
Then I can smile at Satan's rage,
And face a frowning world.

Let cares, like a wild deluge, come,
And storms of sorrow fall;
May I but safely reach my home,
My God, my heaven, my all—

There shall I bathe my weary soul
In seas of heavenly rest,
And not a wave of trouble roll
Across my peaceful breast.

ONCE MORE OUR YOUTHFUL THRONG.

[From the Golden Censer, page 122.]

Once more our youthful throng
In sweetest union raise
To God our choral song
Of gratitude and praise.
When shall we join the holy angels,
Tuning their harps on yonder happy shore?
When in the smiling fields of Eden,
When shall we meet the loved ones gone before?
Hallelujah, sweetly singing,
Through eternal ages ringing,
Hallelujah, Hallelujah,
Praises to the Lamb.

From yonder world of light
Our Father bends His ear,
With angels robed in white,
Our grateful song to hear.
When shall we join, etc.

His eye, that never sleeps,
 With ever watchful care,
His faithful children keeps
 From each besetting snare.
  When shall we join, etc.

Dear Saviour, may we rest
 Our hearts, our hopes on thee;
Reposing on thy breast,
 From every danger free.
  When shall we join, etc.

WHILE YOU'RE YOUNG.

[From Happy Voices, page 31.]

Oh wont you be a Christian
 While you're young?
Oh wont you be a Christian
 While you're young?
Don't think it will be better
To delay it until later,
But remember your Creator
 While you're young.

Oh wont you love the Saviour
 While you're young?
For you he left his glory
 And embraced a cross so gory;
Wont you heed the melting story
 While you're young?

Remember, death may find you
 While you're young:
For friends are often weeping,
And the stars their watch are keeping
O'er the grassy graves, where sleeping
 Lie the young.

Oh, walk the path to glory
  While you're young:
And Jesus will befriend you,
And from danger will defend you,
And a peace divine will send you
  While you're young.

Then wont you be a Christian
  While you're young?
Why from the future borrow,
When, ere comes another morrow,
You may weep in endless sorrow
  While you're young?

WILL YOU MEET US?

[From Happy Voices, page 108.]

Say, brothers, will you meet us,
Say, brothers, will you meet us,
Say, brothers, will you meet us,
  On Canaan's happy shore?

By the grace of God we'll meet you,
By the grace of God we'll meet you,
By the grace of God we'll meet you,
  Where parting is no more.

Jesus lives and reigns forever,
Jesus lives and reigns forever,
Jesus lives and reigns forever,
  On Canaan's happy shore.

Glory, glory, hallelujah,
Glory, glory, hallelujah,
Glory, glory, hallelujah,
  Forever, evermore.

THE GOSPEL BANNER.

[From Happy Voices, page 128.]

Now be the gospel banner
  In every land unfurled,
And be the shout Hosanna
  Re-echoed through the world:
Till every isle and nation,
  Till every tribe and tongue,
Receive the great salvation,
  And join the happy throng.

Yes, thou shalt reign forever,
  O Jesus, King of kings!
Thy light, thy love, thy favor
  Each ransomed captive sings:
The isles for thee are waiting,
  The deserts learn thy praise,
The hills and valleys greeting,
  The song responsive raise.

O, SAY, WILL YOU BE THERE?

[From the New Golden Chain, page 108.]

Beyond this life of hopes and fears,
Beyond this world of griefs and tears,
  There is a region fair.
It knows no change and no decay,
No night, but one unending day.
    Oh say, will you be there?
    Oh say, will you be there?
    Oh say, oh say, oh say, will you be there?

Its glorious gates are closed to sin;
Nought that defiles can enter in
  To mar its beauty rare.
Upon that bright, eternal shore,
Earth's bitter curse is known no more.
    Oh say, will you be there?

No drooping form, no tearful eye,
No hoary head, no weary sigh,
  No pain, no grief, no care;
But joys which mortals may not know,
Like a calm river, ever flow.
    Oh say, will you be there?

Our Saviour, once as mortal child,
As mortal man, by man reviled,
  There many crowns doth wear;
While thousand thousands swell the strain
Of glory to the Lamb once slain!
    Oh say, will you be there?

Who shall be there?   The lowly here—
All those who serve the Lord in fear,
  The world's proud mockery dare:
Who, by the Holy Spirit led,
Rejoice the narrow path to tread:—
    Oh, they shall all be there!
    Oh say, will you be there?

Those who have learnt at Jesus' cross
All earthly gain to count but loss,
  So that his love they share;
Who, gazing on the Crucified,
By faith can say, "For me he died;"
    Oh, they shall all be there!
    Oh say, will you be there?

Will you be there?   You shall, you must,
If, hating sin, in Christ you trust,
  Who did that place prepare.
Still doth his voice sound sweetly, "Come!
I am the way—I'll lead you home—
    With me, you shall be there!"
    Oh say, will you be there?

WE WON'T GIVE UP THE BIBLE.

[From Happy Voices, page 72.]

We won't give up the Bible,
  God's holy book of truth,
The blessed staff of hoary age,
  The guide of early youth,
The lamp which sheds a glorious light
  O'er every dreary road,
The voice which speaks a Saviour's love,
  And leads us home to God.
    We won't give up the Bible,
    God's holy book of truth,
    The blessed staff of hoary age,
    The guide of early youth.

We won't give up the Bible,
  For it alone can tell
The way to save our ruined souls
  From perishing in hell.
And it alone can tell us how
  We can have hopes of heaven,
That through the Saviour's precious blood
  Our sins may be forgiven.
    We won't give up the Bible, etc.

We won't give up the Bible,
  We'll shout it far and wide,
Until the echo shall be heard
  Beyond the rolling tide;
Till all shall know that we, though young,
  Withstand each treach'rous art,
And that from God's own sacred word
  We'll never, never part.
    We won't give up the Bible, etc.

CHRISTMAS CAROL.

[From Happy Voices, page 161.]

We three kings of Orient are;
Bearing gifts we traverse afar
   Field and fountain,
   Moor and mountain,
Following yonder star.
      Oh, star of wonder, star of night,
      Star with royal beauty bright,
      Westward leading,
      Still proceeding,
      Guide us to the perfect light.

Born a King on Bethlehem's plain,
Gold I bring to crown him again—
   King forever,
   Ceasing never
Over us all to reign.
      Oh, star of wonder, star of night, etc.

Frankincense to offer have I:
Incense owns a deity nigh;
   Prayer and praising
   All men raising,
Worship him, God on high.
      Oh, star of wonder, star of night, etc.

Myrrh is mine: its bitter perfume
Breathes a life of gath'ring gloom—
   Sorrowing, sighing,
   Bleeding, dying,
Sealed in the stone-cold tomb.
      Oh, star of wonder, star of night, etc.

Glorious now behold him arise,
King and God and Sacrifice;
  Heaven singing
  Hallelujah;
Joyous the earth replies.
    Oh, star of wonder, star of night, etc.

CHRIST OUR REFUGE.

[From Happy Voices, page 56.]

Jesus, lover of my soul,
  Let me to thy bosom fly,
While the billows near me roll,
  While the tempest still is high;
Hide me, oh my Saviour, hide,
  Till the storm of life is past;
Safe into the haven guide;
  Oh receive my soul at last.

Other refuge have I none;
  Hangs my helpless soul on thee;
Leave, ah, leave me not alone,
  Still support and comfort me:
All my trust on thee is stayed,
  All my help from thee I bring;
Cover my defenseless head
  With the shadow of thy wing.

Thou, O Christ, art all I want;
  More than all in thee I find:
Raise the fallen, cheer the faint,
  Heal the sick, and lead the blind.
Just and holy is thy name,
  I am all unrighteousness;
Vile and full of sin I am,
  Thou art full of truth and grace.

YOUTHFUL MARINER.

[From Happy Voices, page 88.]

Down the stream of life they glide,
    Little mariners so frail ;
Gently heaves the swelling tide,
    Softly blows the fav'ring gale.
They suspect no danger nigh,
Cloudless is the summer sky ;
Joy lights up each youthful eye
    As they gaily sail.

But the angry storm may blow,
    And the smiling heavens grow dark ;
And the hidden rocks below
    Rudely tear the trembling bark ;
Oft upon the listening ear
Falls the shriek of wild despair,
From the shipwrecked mariner
    In his shattered bark.

Heavenly Pilot, be our guide,
    Youthful mariners defend ;
O'er the winds and waves preside,
    In the dangerous hour befriend ;
Thou who bad'st the tempest cease,
And from peril didst release,
Guide them to the port of peace,
    Where their fears shall end.

HAPPY GREETING TO ALL.

[From the Oriola, page 63.]

Come, children, and join in our festival song,
And hail the sweet joys which this day brings along ;
We'll join our glad voices in one hymn of praise
To God, who has kept us, and lengthened our days.
    Happy greeting to all.

Our Father in heaven, we lift up to thee
Our voice of thanksgiving, our glad jubilee;
Oh, bless us, and guide us, dear Saviour we pray,
That from thy blessed precepts we never may stray.
　　　　Happy greeting to all.

And if, ere this year has drawn to a close,
Some loved one among us in death shall repose,
Grant, Lord, that the spirit in heaven may dwell,
In the bosom of Jesus, where all shall be well.
　　　　Happy greeting to all.

Kind teachers, we children would thank you this day,
That faithfully, kindly, you've taught us the way,
How we may escape from the world's sinful charms,
And find a safe refuge in Jesus' loved arms.
　　　　Happy greeting to all.

PENITENCE.

[From the Oriola, page 201.]

Take my heart, Oh Father! take it;
　　Make and keep it all thine own:
Let thy spirit melt and break it;
　　Turn to flesh this heart of stone.
Heavenly Father, deign to mould it
　　In obedience to thy will;
And, as passing years unfold it,
　　Keep it meek and childlike still.

Father, make it pure and lowly,
　　Peaceful, kind, and far from strife,
Turning from the paths unholy
　　Of this vain and sinful life.
May the blood of Jesus heal it,
　　And its sins be all forgiven:
Holy Spirit, take and seal it;
　　Guide it in the path to heaven.

JOYFUL BE OUR NUMBERS.

[From the Oriola, page 229.]

Joyful, joyful, joyful be our numbers,
 Bursting forth the soul-enlivening lay,
Swell the strain to music's sweetest murmurs,
 Every heart now hail this happy day,
Bursting forth the soul-enlivening lay,
 Hail! O hail! this happy, happy day.

From the hill and valley far away,
We come with merry greetings in our lay.

Often as our festal day rolls round,
We hail it ever with harmonious sound.

Golden hours are fleeting, like a spell,
We meet, too soon to part and say farewell.

Give the hand of friendship ere we part,
May Heaven now embalm it in each heart.

THE SABBATH SCHOOL.

[From the Oriola, page 107.]

The Sabbath school's a place of prayer,
 I love to meet my teachers there,
 I love to meet my teachers there.
They teach me there that every one,
 May find, in heaven, a happy home,
 May find in heaven a happy home.
  I love to go—I love to go—
  I love to go to Sabbath school.
  I love to go—I love to go—
  I love to go to Sabbath school.

In God's own book we're taught to read
  How Christ for sinners groan'd and bled,
That precious blood a ransom gave,
  For sinful man—his soul to save.
    I love to go—I love to go—
    I love to go to Sabbath school.

In Sabbath school we sing and pray,
  And learn to love the Sabbath day;
That, when on earth our Sabbaths end,
  A glorious rest in heaven we'll spend.
    I love to go—I love to go—
    I love to go to Sabbath school.

And when our days on earth are o'er,
  We'll meet in heaven to part no more;
Our teachers kind we there shall greet,
  And oh! what joy 't will be to meet
    In heaven above—in heaven above—
    In heaven above, to part no more.

KIND WORDS CAN NEVER DIE.

[From the Oriola, page 146.]

Kind words can never die,
  Cherished and blest,
God knows how deep they lie
  Stored in the breast:
Like childhood's simple rhymes,
Said o'er a thousand times,
Age in all years and climes,
  Distant and near.
Kind words can never die,
  Never die, never die,
Kind words can never die,
  No, never, never die.

Childhood can never die—
  Wrecks of the past,
Float o'er the memory,
  Bright to the last:
Many a happy thing,
Many a daisy spring
Float o'er life's ceaseless wing,
  Far, far away.
Childhood can never die,
  Never die, never die,
Childhood can never die,
  No, never, never die.

Sweet thoughts can never die,
  Though, like the flowers,
Their brightest hues may fly,
  In wintry hours;
But when the gentle dew
Gives them their charms anew
With many an added hue,
  They bloom again.
Sweet thoughts can never die,
  Never die, never die,
Sweet thoughts can never die,
  No, never, never die.

Our souls can never die,
  Though in the tomb
We may all have to lie,
  Wrapped in its gloom:
What though the flesh decay,
Souls pass in peace away,
Live through eternal day,
  With Christ above.
Our souls can never die,
  Never die, never die,
Our souls can never die,
  No, never, never die.

THE BRIGHT CROWN.

[From the Oriola, page 180.]

Ye valiant soldiers of the cross,
  Ye, happy, praying band,
Though in this world you suffer loss,
  You'll reach fair Canaan's land;
Let us never mind the scoffs nor the frowns of the
    world,
For we've all got the cross to bear,
It will only make the crown the brighter to shine,
When we have the crown to wear.

All earthly pleasures we'll forsake,
  When heaven appears in view,
In Jesus' strength we'll undertake
    To fight our passage through.
      Let us never, etc.

O, what a glorious shout there'll be,
  When we arrive at home,
Our friends and Jesus we shall see,
  And God shall say " Well done."
    Let us never, etc.

COME AND SING.

[From the Oriola, page 78.]

Come, and sing with joy and gladness,
  Elevate your hearts in praise;
Come, dismiss all gloom and sadness,
  High your songs exulting raise,
With th' angelic choirs uniting,
  Sing of Jesus' wondrous love;
'Tis a subject so delighting,
  Thrilling all the harps above.

  14

Come, and sweetly tune your voices,
  Raise them to a lofty strain;
Sing aloud, while Heaven rejoices,
  Shout! for Jesus comes to reign;
Glory, hear the angels crying,
  Glory to the Saviour's name;
Shall not children, with them vieing,
  Here on earth his praise proclaim.

Yes! it was the Saviour's pleasure
  That they should not hold their peace:
And his blessings, without measure,
  He bestowed on such as these:
Then to heaven high ascending,
  Shall our anthems quickly rise;
With angelic voices blending,
  Far above the azure skies.

ALL-SUFFICIENCY OF JESUS.

[From the Oriola, page 91.]

How tedious and tasteless the hours
  When Jesus no longer I see!
Sweet prospects, sweet birds, and sweet flowers,
  Have all lost their sweetness to me;
The midsummer sun shines but dim,
  The fields strive in vain to look gay;
But when I am happy in him,
  December's as pleasant as May.

His name yields the richest perfume,
  And sweeter than music his voice;
His presence disperses my gloom,
  And makes all within me rejoice.
I should, were he always thus nigh,
  Have nothing to wish or to fear;
No mortal so happy as I—
  My summer would last all the year

My Lord, if indeed I am thine,
  If thou art my sun and my song,
Then, why do I languish and pine?
  And why are my winters so long?
Oh, drive these dark clouds from my sky;
  Thy soul-cheering presence restore;
Or take me up to thee on high,
  Where winter and clouds are no more.

JESUS EVER NEAR.

[From the Oriola, page 105.]

Dear Saviour, ever at my side,
  How loving thou must be
To leave thy home in heaven to guard
  A little child like me.
Thy beautiful and shining face
  I see not, though so near;
The sweetness of thy soft low voice
  I am too deaf to hear.

I cannot feel thee touch my hand
  With pressure light and mild,
To check me, as my mother did
  When I was but a child.
But I have felt thee in my thoughts
  Fighting with sin for me;
And when my heart loves God, I know
  The sweetness is from thee.

And when, dear Saviour! I kneel down
  Morning and night to prayer,
Something there is within my heart
  Which tells me thou art there.
Yes! when I pray, thou prayest, too—
  Thy prayer is all for me;
But when I sleep, thou sleepest not
  But watchest patiently.

ACROSS THE RIVER.

[From Fresh Laurels, page 8.]

Ah, yes! there's a fairer zone,
Where sin and sorrow are unknown;
Where weary souls find peaceful rest,
And all that love the Lord are blest.
  'Tis just across the river,
  The narrow, narrow river,
  'Tis just across the river
  Upon the other shore;
  And there upon the other shore
  We hope to meet to part no more,
  And dwell with God forever,
  And dwell with God forever.

Ah, yes! there's a purer clime,
Beyond the clouds that darken Time;
A world of perfect joy and love,
Where saints and angels live above.
  'Tis just across the river, etc.

Then gird up our loins and go,
Forsaking all things here below;
No earthly pleasure can compare,
With bliss we may in heaven share.
  'Tis just across the river, etc.

THE THRONE OF GRACE.

[From Fresh Laurels, page 13.]

Sweet is the precious gift of prayer,
  To bow before a throne of grace;
To leave our every burden there,
  And gain new strength to run our race;
To gird our heavenly armor on,
Depending on the Lord alone.

And sweet the whisper of his love,
  When conscience sinks beneath its load,
That bids our guilty fears remove,
  And points to Christ's atoning blood.
Oh then 'tis sweet indeed to know
God can be just and gracious too.

Sweet is the peace that Jesus gives
  When all around is dressed in gloom;
'Tis sweet to know the Saviour lives
  When friends are hurried to the tomb,
And those we love are snatched away
Like flowers that wither in a day.

But, O, to see our Saviour's face,
  From sin and sorrow to be freed,
To dwell in his divine embrace—
  This will be sweeter far indeed!
The fairest form of earthly bliss
Is less than nought, compared with this.

THE GOLDEN RULE.

[From Fresh Laurels, page 28.]

While our hearts are light, and our homes are bright,
  And the sun is smiling o'er us,
We come to learn of a brighter path,
  To a better land before us;
Of a royal road to that blest abode,
  Of love and joy and beauty,
And the golden rule of our Sunday school
  Is the upward path of duty.
    We will follow the Golden Rule,
    We will follow the Golden Rule,
    We will follow, follow, follow, follow,
    Follow the Golden Rule.

We will love our neighbors as ourselves,
We will treat them like our brothers,
And as we wish they should do to us,
So we will do to others.
And thus obey from day to day
That law so full of beauty,
For the Golden Rule of our Sunday school
Is the royal road of duty.
We will follow the Golden Rule, etc.

GLADLY MEETING.

[From Fresh Laurels, page 25.]

Gladly meeting,
Kindly greeting,
On this holy Sabbath day,
Sinful thoughts be all forsaken,
Every seat in quiet taken,
Let each heart to God awaken,
While we sing and pray.

Gladly meeting,
Kindly greeting,
Let us all unite in heart,
While the throne we're all addressing,
And our sinful ways confessing,
Let us seek a heavenly blessing,
Ere we here depart.

Gladly meeting,
Kindly greeting,
As each Sabbath shall return,
May our minds by study brighten,
May our aspirations heighten,
And may grace our souls enlighten,
While we strive to learn.

WATCH AND PRAY.

[From Fresh Laurels, page 54.]

Watch, for the time is short;
  Watch, while 'tis called to-day;
Watch, lest the world prevail;
  Watch, christian, watch and pray;
Watch, for the flesh is weak;
  Watch, for the foe is strong;
Watch, lest the bridegroom come;
  Watch, though He tarry long.
      O, watch and pray,
      O, watch and pray,
      O, watch and pray,
      O, watch and pray,
      O, watch in the darkness,
      And watch in the day;
      Christian, watch and pray.

Chase slumber from thine eyes;
  Chase doubting from thy breast;
Thine is the promised prize
  Of heaven's eternal rest;
Watch, christian, watch and pray;
  Thy Saviour watched for thee;
Till from his brow they poured
  Great drops of agony.
      O, watch and pray, etc.

Take Jesus for thy trust;
  Watch, watch forever more;
Watch, for thou soon must sleep
  With thousands gone before;
Now, when thy sun is up,
  Now, while 'tis called to-day,
Now is accepted time;
  Watch, christian, watch and pray.
      O, watch and pray, etc.

JEWELS.

[From Fresh Laurels, page 65.]

When He cometh, when He cometh,
  To make up his jewels,
All his jewels, precious jewels,
  His loved and his own.
    Like the stars of the morning,
    His bright crown adorning,
    They shall shine in their beauty,
    Bright gems for his crown.

He will gather, He will gather,
  The gems for his kingdom;
All the pure ones, all the bright ones,
  His lov'd and his own.
    Like the stars, etc.

Little children, little children,
  Who love their Redeemer,
Are the jewels, precious jewels,
  His loved and his own.
    Like the stars, etc.

THE BEAUTIFUL TREE OF LIFE.

[From Fresh Laurels, page 15.]

On a hill stands a beautiful tree,
  Its fruit is all golden and fair,
And its shade and its treasures are free,
  For all who may thither repair,
Its leaves, ever green, do not die,
  Its flowers with fragrance abound,
Its splendor enraptures the eye,
  Its branches with music resound.
  Its branches with music resound.

Though thousands by night and by day
  Have feasted and gathered in store,
Have borne its rich bounties away
  Its fullness remains evermore,
O, what is its name? who can tell?
  And the hill, where, O, where can it be?
By thy side I will haste me to dwell,
  O wonderful—beautiful tree.

On Zion's fair mount you behold
  Its form in bright grandeur arise,
There glitter its green and its gold,
  There lifts its tall head to the skies:
'Twas planted by Infinite love,
  From the hills everlasting it came,
Truth Eternal, they call it above;
  But, Bible, on earth, is its name.

WELCOME TO THE SABBATH.

[From Fresh Laurels, page 55.]

Welcome, welcome, day of rest,
  Sweet relief from every care,
Grateful to the weary breast
  Are the joys thy moments bear;
God of love, thy grace impart,
  Comfort every mourning heart,
God of love, thy grace impart,
  Comfort every mourning heart.

Welcome, welcome, Sabbath bells,
  Chiming on the fragrant air,
Pealing o'er the flowery dells,
  Calling to the house of prayer:
Those who long the way have trod,
Those who love to worship God.

Precious words of life we hear,
　From our pastor's lips they fall,
Strains of music greet our ear,
　Lord, we praise thy name for all;
On the wings of faith we rise
Upward to our native skies.

When these mortal scenes decay,
　When the toils of earth are past,
Jesus, may we hear thee say,
　"Welcome, faithful ones, at last;
Of my Father you are blest,
Enter now eternal rest."

TRAVELING HOME.

[From Fresh Laurels, page 70.]

Saviour, thy word a lamp shall be,
　Guiding my feet to Zion;
Lighting the path that leads to thee,
　Cheering the way to Zion.
　　Traveling home, traveling home,
　　Traveling home to Zion;
　　Traveling home, we're traveling home
　　To dwell forever more.

Saviour, I tread the heavenly road,
　Singing and filled with pleasure;
Looking by faith to thine abode,
　Seeking a glorious treasure.
　　Traveling home, etc.

When I am weak and tempted here,
　Lonely my way pursuing,
Saviour, I know, I feel thee near,
　Vigor and strength renewing.
　　Traveling home, etc.

Saviour, with all thy saints above,
  Close by the shining river;
Soon shall I meet the friends I love,
  Singing thy praise forever.
    Traveling home, etc.

LIGHT AND COMFORT.

[From Fresh Laurels, page 35.]

Light and Comfort of my soul,
When the billows o'er me roll;
Thou dost bid me in thy word,
Cast my burden on the Lord,
Jesus, Saviour once betrayed,
Sacrifice for sinners made;
Wretched, lost, to thee I fly,
Save, O save me, or I die.

Lord, my soul in tears would mourn,
All the anguish thou hast borne,
In the garden I would be,
Lonely watcher still with thee.
Thou hast suffered, thou hast bled,
Thorns have pierced thy sacred head,
Jesus, while I cling to thee,
Let thy sorrow plead for me.

Mocked and scourged—condemned to die,
On the cross extended high;
Tenant of the lonely tomb,
Mighty conqueror o'er its gloom,
Crowned victorious God of love,
To thy Father's home above:
Grant my soul a place at last,
When the storms of life are past.

ENCOURAGEMENT.

[From Fresh Laurels, page 58.]

O teacher, sad and weary,
    Because thy work seems vain,
Look from thyself to Jesus,
    And thou wilt hope again.
Perchance thou art discouraged,
    That yet no fruit appears;
But ere the joyful harvest,
    The seed is sown in tears.
        Sown in tears, sown in tears,
        The seed is sown in tears.

Hast thou so soon forgotten
    The promise of thy Lord,
That none for him who labor
    Shall fail of their reward!
If thus thou pray and labor,
    Immortal souls to win,
Thou at thy Lord's appearing,
    Bright as the stars shall shine,
    Bright as the stars shall shine.

IF WE KNEW.

[From Fresh Laurels, page 56.]

If we knew when walking thoughtless
    Through the crowded, noisy way,
That some pearl of wondrous whiteness
    Close beside our pathway lay,
We would pause when now we hasten,
    We would often look around,
Lest our careless feet should trample
    Some rare jewel in the ground.
        Lest our careless feet should trample,
    · Some rare jewel in the ground.

If we knew what forms were fainting
     ' For the shade that we should fling,
If we knew what lips were parching
     For the water we should bring,
We would haste with eager footsteps,
     We would work with willing hands,
Bearing cups of cooling water,
     Planting rows of shading palms.

If we knew when friends around us,
     Closely press to say " good bye."
Which among the lips that kiss us,
     First should 'neath the daisies lie,
We would clasp our arms around them,
     Looking on them through our tears,
Tender words of love eternal
     We would whisper in their ears.

If we knew what lives were darkened
     By some thoughtless word of ours,
Which had ever lain upon them,
     Like the frost upon the flowers,
O with what sincere repentings,
     With what anguish of regret,
While our eyes were overflowing,
     We would cry, " forgive," " forget."

If we knew ! alas ! and do we
     Ever care or seek to know,
Whether bitter herbs or roses
     In our neighbors' gardens grow?
God forgive us! lest hereafter
     Our hearts break to hear him say
" Careless child, I never knew you,
     From my presence flee away."

JERUSALEM THE GOLDEN.

[From Fresh Laurels, page 87.]

Jerusalem the golden,
  With milk and honey blest,
Beneath thy contemplation
  Sink heart and voice to rest.
I know not—Oh! I know not
  What joys await me there,
What radiancy of glory,
  What bliss beyond compare.

They stand, those halls of Zion,
  All jubilant with song,
And bright with many an angel,
  And all the martyr throng.
There is the throne of David,
  And there, from toil released,
The shout of them that triumph,
  The song of them that feast.

And they who, with their Leader,
  Have conquered in the fight,
Forever and forever
  Are clad in robes of white.
Oh, land that seest no sorrow,
  Oh, state that fear'st no strife,
Oh, royal land of flowers,
  Oh, realms and home of life!

Oh, sweet and blessed country,
  The home of God's elect,
Oh, sweet and blessed country,
  That eager hearts expect!
Jesus, in mercy bring us
  To that dear land of rest,
Who art, with God the Father
  And Spirit, ever blest.

LORD'S DAY.

[From Fresh Laurels, page 88.]

Christ, the Lord is risen to-day,
 Glory hallelujah!
Our triumphant holy day,
 Hallelujah, praise the Lord.
He who died upon the cross,
 Glory hallelujah!
Suffered to redeem our loss,
 Hallelujah, praise the Lord!
 Hallelujah! hallelujah!
 Praise ye the Lord.

Love's redeeming work is done,
 Glory hallelujah!
Fought the fight, the battle won:
 Hallelujah, praise the Lord.
Lo! the sun's eclipse is o'er,
 Glory hallelujah!
Lo! he sets in blood no more,
 Hallelujah, praise the Lord!
 Hallelujah! etc.

Vain the stone, the watch, the seal,
 Christ has burst the gates of hell:
Death in vain forbids his rise;
 Christ hath opened Paradise.
 Hallelujah! etc.

Lives again our glorious King;
 Where, O death, is now thy sting?
Once he died our souls to save;
 Where's thy vict'ry, boasting grave?
 Hallelujah! etc.

Arise, arise, poor sinner,
  The Spirit bids you come
And seek in heaven a land of rest,
  Sweet land of rest,
The christian's native home.

Arise, arise, poor sinner,
  Your Father's voice now hear;
He says your sins are all forgiven,
  All, all forgiven;
My son, be of good cheer.

COME, O COME.

[From Fresh Laurels, page 80.]

Come, O come, our festive day returning,
  Filled with joy, its rosy light we see;
God of love, our hearts with rapture burning,
  Breathe, in a grateful song, our homage to thee.
    Here once again our mingled voices swelling;
    Here with delight we love thy praise to sing.
    We will rejoice, of all thy goodness telling,
    Oh, be thou exalted high, our Saviour and King.

Come, O come, the flowers with verdure teeming,
  Bless the hand that made the forms so gay;
Come, O come, the sun with luster beaming,
  Crowns with a happy smile our high festive day.
    Here once again, etc.

Come, O Come, the day is now before us,
  Not a cloud to dim its golden ray;
Angel eyes from heaven are bending o'er us,
  Gilding the tranquil hours with joy while they stay.
    Here once again, etc.

SABBATH SCHOOL PRAYER.

[From Fresh Laurels, page 99.]

How great is the blessing of Sabbath school prayer,
And how good for the christian it is to be there;
Away from temptation, from error and wrong,
Where the mourner finds comfort, the weak are made
    strong;
The blessed place of prayer, 'tis sweet to be there.

We read in the Bible that prayer shall prevail,
That with earnest petition no good thing shall fail;
Then is it not precious when burdened with care,
To enjoy the rich blessing of Sabbath school prayer?
The blessed place of prayer, 'tis sweet to be there.

Let teachers and scholars look upward to-day,
And give thanks to the Father who taught them to pray;
Who gives them all favor, but none to compare
With the heavenly blessing of Sabbath school prayer.
The blessed place of prayer, 'tis sweet to be there.

PISGAH'S MOUNTAIN.

[From Fresh Laurels, page 78.]

Joyful away to Pisgah's mountain,
    Borne on the wings of faith we soar,
Sweetly we hear the echo ringing,
    Happy voices on the other shore.
Hark! they sing in the bright vales of Eden,
    Songs of praise to the Lamb that was slain;
Round his throne with the martyrs they gather
    There united forever to reign.
        Would you sit by the banks of the river
        With the friends you have loved by your side,
        Would you join in the songs of the angels?
        Then be ready to follow your guide.

Christians, behold the hill of Zion,
　　See where our purest treasure lies.
Work for the Lord whate'er our trials,
　　O, be faithful, we shall win the prize.
Crowned with light in a mansion of beauty,
　　We shall dwell with the pure and the blest,
We shall sing with the faithful in glory,
　　Where the weary forever shall rest.
　　　　Would you sit, etc.

We're pressing on with eager longing,
　　Pressing toward the swelling tide;
Jesus will bear us safely over,
　　We shall anchor on the other side.
Saved by grace to his kingdom exalted,
　　When the billows of Jordan are passed,
We shall sing with the friends we have cherished,
　　Glory, glory, we're home, home at last.
　　　　Would you sit, etc.

GRAND MILLENIUM SONG.

[From Fresh Laurels, page 90.]

Rejoice, rejoice, the promised time is coming,
　　Rejoice, rejoice, the wilderness shall bloom,
Rejoice, rejoice, the promised time is coming,
　　Rejoice, rejoice, the wilderness shall bloom,
And Zion's children then shall sing,
　　"The deserts all are blossoming:"
Rejoice, rejoice, the promised time is coming,
　　Rejoice, rejoice, the wilderness shall bloom,
The Gospel banner, wide unfurled,
　　Shall wave in triumph o'er the world;
And every creature, bond and free,
　　Shall hail the glorious jubilee.

Rejoice, rejoice, the promised time is coming,
  Rejoice, rejoice, Jerusalem shall sing;
From Zion shall the law go forth,
  And all shall hear from south to north:
Rejoice, rejoice, the promised time is coming,
  Rejoice, rejoice, Jerusalem shall sing;
And truth shall sit on every hill,
  And blessings flow in every rill,
And praise shall every heart employ,
  And every voice shall shout with joy:
Rejoice, rejoice, the promised time is coming,
  Rejoice, rejoice, Jerusalem shall sing.

Rejoice, rejoice, the promised time is coming,
  Rejoice, rejoice, the Prince of Peace shall reign,
And lambs shall with the leopard play,
  For nought shall harm in Zion's way:
Rejoice, rejoice, the promised time is coming,
  Rejoice, rejoice, the Prince of Peace shall reign.
The sword and spear, of needless worth,
  Shall prune the tree and plough the earth,
And peace shall smile from shore to shore,
  And nations shall learn war no more:
Rejoice, rejoice, the promised time is coming,
  Rejoice, rejoice, the Prince of Peace shall reign.

THE PORT OF PEACE.

[From Fresh Laurels, page 106.]

Where, O where, is yon vessel going,
  See her now on the waters blue;
All her sails in the breeze are floating,
  Hear the song of her gallant crew.
    Haste on board, 'tis the Captain calling,
    We are waiting, we are waiting,
    Precious souls we are bearing onward,
    Joyful to the port of peace,
    Joyful to the blessed port of peace.

Millions now to that vessel flocking,
　　Young and old on the deck they stand;
Yet there's room and a hearty welcome,
　　Passage free to the promised land.
　　　Haste on board, etc.

Praise the Lord, 'tis the old ship Zion,
　　Jesus is her Captain's name;
Colors bright from her mast are flying,
　　We have heard of her noble fame.
　　　Haste on board, etc.

Quick! on board, she has weigh'd her anchor,
　　Quick! on board, for the wind is fair;
World adieu, we are sailing onward,
　　Heaven's our home, and our hearts are there.
　　　Haste on board, etc.

EVENING PRAYER.

[From Fresh Laurels, page 103.]

Jesus, tender Shepherd, hear us;
　　Bless thy little lambs to-night:
Through the darkness be thou near us:
　　Keep us safe till morning light.

All this day thy hand has led us,
　　And we thank thee for thy care;
Thou hast clothed us, warmed us, fed us,
　　Listen to our evening prayer!

May our sins be all forgiven;
　　Bless the friends we love so well;
Take us, when we die, to heaven,
　　Happy there with thee to dwell.

A SABBATH SCHOOL IN HEAVEN.

[From Fresh Laurels, page 118.]

Dear Father, grant our earnest prayer,
　While here we meekly bow before thee,
That those committed to our care
　May in a brighter world adore thee:
And should the sweet and glorious sound
　Of " welcome home" to us be given ;
Oh, what a glorious sight 'twould be
　To see our Sabbath-school in heaven,
To see our Sabbath-school in heaven.

Oh, may we true and faithful prove,
　To those young souls so weak and tender,
That we in that eternal day,
　To God a just account may render:
And when we lay us down to die,
　And life's frail cord at last is riven ;
May we with shining garments meet
　This much lov'd Sabbath-school in heaven,
This much lov'd Sabbath-school in heaven.

THE HAPPY TIME.

[From Fresh Laurels, page 119.]

O the happy time is coming
　When the gospel trumpet's sound,
Shall be heard by every nation,
　To the earth's remotest bound·
When the vale shall be exalted,
　And the verdant hills rejoice,
And the ocean join the chorus,
　With a loud triumphant voice.
　　Lo ! the morning light will break,
　　And the day is drawing nigh,
　　Yes, a glorious time is coming soon,
　　We shall hail it by and by.

O the happy time is coming
  When the cry of war shall cease,
And the standard of our Saviour,
  Be the olive branch of peace ;
Underneath our vine and fig tree
  We will never be afraid,
There is none will dare molest us,
  In their calm and quiet shade.
    Lo! the morning light will break, etc.

O the happy time is coming
  By our fathers once foretold,
It is promised in the Bible,
  It was sung by prophets old :
They who sit in heathen darkness,
  Soon the morning light shall see,
And the world with songs of triumph,
  Hail the glorious jubilee.
    Lo! the morning light will break, etc.

WHAT SHALL I DO WITH JESUS?

[From Fresh Laurels, page 116.]

What shall I do with Jesus,
  The Christ who may be mine?
Accept him as my Saviour,
  Or spurn the gift divine?
His only Son God gave me—
  I must, I do decide;
And Christ I take to save me,
  Or Christ is now denied.
    "What shall I do with Jesus?"
    I'll give my heart to Jesus!
    Upon the tree on Calvary,
    He gave his life for me.

What shall I do with Jesus.
  The precious Lamb of God?
I cast my soul upon him—
  He bathes it in his blood;
I'll gratefully confess him
  Before the vile and just;
My ransomed powers shall bless him,
  My sure and only trust.
    " What shall I do with Jesus?" etc.

What shall I do with Jesus?
  For him the cross I'll take;
All earthly losses suffer,
  Ere I the Lord forsake
In scenes of joy and sighing,
  His love shall be the same;
While living and in dying
  I'll glory in his name.
    " What shall I do with Jesus?" otc.

What now I do with Jesus,
  When this brief life is past,
With me will be remembered
  Before his bar at last.
He will not then disown me
  With those who hate and scoff;
At his right hand he'll crown me—
  He will not cast me off.
    " What shall I do with Jesus?" etc.

JACOB'S PRAYER.

[From Fresh Laurels. page 92.]

All night long till break of day,
  Jacob wept his bitter prayer,
Till the Angel on his way,
  Christ the Angel blest him there.

I'm a needy sinner too,
  Torn with anguish, guilt and fears,
I to Jesus too will go,
  Go and bathe his feet with tears.

Jesus, at thy cross I lie
  All night long till break of day;
Perish here if I must die—
  Unforgiven, go not away.
Saviour, wilt thou take my heart?
  It is all I have to give.
Sin-defiled in every part,
  Such a gift wilt thou receive?

Oh, how kindly Jesus spake:
  " Go in peace—all is forgiven.
Wilt thou all for me forsake,
  Love, and follow me to heaven?"
Jesus, I thy goodness bless,
  And with wondering love adore;
Let me never love thee less,
  Let me love thee more and more.

DEDICATION HYMN.

[From Fresh Laurels, page 96.]

We dedicate to Jesus
  Our pleasant Sabbath home;
'Twas ours, we freely give it
  To him, and Him alone.
And O, whene'er we gather
  Within these sacred walls,
Be His the smile that greets us,
  And His the voice that calls,
Be His the smile that greets us,
  And His the voice that calls.

'Tis strange the King of Glory,
   The Head of Angel Bands,
Should deign to dwell among us
   In temples made with hands.
But we have felt his presence
   And still the promise claim,
That he will be wherever
   We gather in his name.

We give ourselves to Jesus,
   Our talents and our time;
Thy tender love constrains us,
   And we would fain be thine.
O give us strength to labor
   Till life's brief hour is past,
And grant each child and teacher
   A starry crown at last.

BLESSED ARE THE PEOPLE.

[From Fresh Laurels, page 100.]

Blessed are the people that know the joyful sound,
Still with peace and plenty they are crowned;
God is ever with them, their refuge and their might,
They shall dwell together in his holy light.
   Praise him ye nations, great is your King;
   Under the shadow of his wing,
   He will keep you safely
   From the tempter's snare,
   Evil cannot harm you,
   Cannot harm you there.

Blessed are the people whose trust is in the Lord,
Walking in the council of his word;
They shall be exalted who love his holy name,
They shall never, never seek his face in vain.
   Praise him ye nations, etc.

Blessed are the people who on his arm repose,
Looking to the hills whence comfort flows;
They shall grow and flourish who in his strength abide,
Like the trees that blossom by the river's side.
    Praise him ye nations, etc.

Blessed are the people who know the joyful sound,
Still with peace and plenty they are crowned:
God is ever with them, their refuge and their might,
They shall dwell together in his holy light.
    Praise him ye nations, etc.

THE SHINING HILLS OF GLORY.

[From Fresh Laurels, page 117.]

O come to the hills of glory,
   And leave this gloomy vale of sin,
The gate of grace stands open,
   And you may enter in.
     The shining hills of glory,
     How brightly do they stand,
     We'll soon be there together,
     All safe at God's right hand,
     Safe, safe, safe,
     All safe at God's right hand.

O come to the hills of glory,
   O come, where endless pleasures reign,
Lay down your heavy burden
   Of grief, and care, and pain.
     The shining hills of glory, etc.

O come to the hills of glory,
   Why will you linger trifling here,
The blessed Saviour calls you,
   The friend who loves you dear.
     The shining hills of glory, etc.

O come to the hills of glory,
  By angel footsteps gently trod,
There you may dwell forever,
  In blessed peace with God.
    Tho shining hills of glory, etc.

HOLY SABBATH.

[From Fresh Laurels, page 93.]

Holy Sabbath, happy morning,
  Joyfully the bells we hear,
Sweetly calling, gently calling
  Us to praise and prayer.
Sweetly sounding through each street,
  And floating on the quiet air,
Comes the dear familiar greeting,
  Calling us to prayer.

Holy Sabbath, glad young voices,
  Welcome you with joyous song,
While the aged heart rejoices
  With the youthful throng.
May the light of this blest morning,
  Every youthful heart illume
With a cheerful sacred presence,
  That shall banish gloom.

Basking in the holy radiance
  Of this blessed Sabbath morn,
May the blessed angels keep us,
  Till another dawn.
And when earth's best, purest love-light
  Fadeth from our sight away,
May our risen Saviour take us
  To his endless day.

JOY! JOY! JOY!

[From Fresh Laurels, page 128.]

Joy! joy! joy! there is joy in heaven with the angels;
   Joy! joy! joy! for the prodigal's return!
He has come, he has come,
   To his Father's house at last;
He was lost, he is found,
   And the night of gloom is past.
Blessed hour of joy, and communion sweet,
For his heart is full and his love complete,
His Father sees him and hastes to meet,
   And bid him welcome home.

Joy! joy! joy! in the courts of heaven resounding,
   Joy! joy! joy! o'er the prodigal's return;
Hark! the song, hark! the song,
   'Tis a joyful, joyful strain,
Welcome home, welcome home,
   To thy Father's house again.
While his eye is dim with the falling tears;
Of repentant grief, over wasted years,
The pardoning voice of his Father cheers,
   And bids him welcome home.

Joy! joy! joy! in the radiant fields of glory,
   Joy! joy! joy! when a wandering soul returns;
Let us haste, let us haste,
   While the morning sun is bright,
Jesus calls, Jesus calls,
   To a land of love and light.
We will journey on till our pilgrim feet
Shall be found at last in the golden street,
Our glorious Saviour will smile to greet,
   And bid us welcome home.

I AM WAITING BY THE RIVER.

[From Fresh Laurels, page 125.]

I am waiting by the river,
  And my heart has waited long;
Now I think I hear the chorus
  Of the angels' welcome song,
Oh! I see the dawn is breaking
  On the hill-tops of the blest,
"Where the wicked cease from troubling,
  And the weary are at rest."

Far away beyond the shadows
  Of this weary vale of tears,
There the tide of bliss is sweeping
  Through the bright and changeless years;
Oh! I long to be with Jesus,
  In the mansions of the blest,
"Where the wicked cease from troubling,
  And the weary are at rest."

They are launching on the river,
  From the calm and quiet shore,
And they soon will bear my spirit
  Where the weary sigh no more;
For the tide is swiftly flowing,
  And I long to greet the blest,
"Where the wicked cease from troubling,
  And the weary are at rest."

SABBATH EVENING.

[From the Plymouth, page 127.]

Softly fades the twilight ray,
Of the holy Sabbath day;
Gently as life's setting sun,
When the Christian's course is run,
When the Christian's course is run.
CHORUS—Holy Sabbath, softly fading,
    Gently as life's setting sun.

Night her solemn mantle spreads,
O'er the earth as daylight fades;
All things tell of calm repose,
At the holy Sabbath's close.—CHO.

Saviour, may our Sabbaths be,
Days of peace and joy in thee;
'Till in heaven our souls repose,
Where the Sabbaths ne'er shall close.—CHO.

WANDERING STRANGER.

[From the Sabbath School Bell, No. 2, page 161.]

"Say, whither, wandering stranger,
  Ah! whither dost thou roam?
O'er this wide world a ranger,
  Hast thou no friend, no home?"
"Yes, I've a Friend who never
  Is absent from my side
And I've a home wherever
  In peace I shall abide."

"But want and woe have driven
  The roses from thy cheek;
And garments rent and riven,
  Thy poverty bespeak."
"I've food with which the angels
  Would all delighted be;
And robes of dazzling brightness
  Are now awaiting me.

"Come, then, benign inquirer,
  And join me on my way;
I'm journeying to a country
  Where beams an endless day;
Where saints and angels, falling
  Before the great, white throne,
To you, to me are calling,
  Haste, pilgrim, hasten home."

OPEN WIDE THE GARDEN GATE.

[From the Plymouth, page 194.]

Open wide the garden gate,
　　Let the little wanderers in ;
Let them now no longer wait,
　　Tho' their lives are soiled by sin.
There is room enough for them
　　In the perfume-laden bowers,
Room for many a sparkling gem
　　'Mid the Gard'ner's living flowers.

Take them from the sin tossed flood,
　　Moor them at the Eden isle ;
Sprinkled with atoning blood,
　　Theirs shall be an angel smile.
Shield them from the world's stern care,
　　Guide their little footsteps right;
Let them breathe the heavenly air,
　　Let them see its living light

Suffer them to come to Him,
　　Shepherd of the cherub band;
He can light the valley dim,
　　Leading from this desert land,
Nurtured with a kindly care,
　　All the weeds of sin kept down,
Golden fruit their lives shall bear,
　　Till they win the sparkling crown.

And with golden harps in hand,
　　Glad'ning all that blest abode,
They shall shine, a star·gem'd band
　　In the coronal of God.
Open, then, the garden gate,
　　Let the little wanderers in;
See the blessed Saviour wait—
　　Wait to save their souls from sin.

16

OUR GLAD VOICES.

[From the Sabbath School Bell, No. 2, page 104.]

Our glad voices let us raise
  In a song of love and praise,
That we're taught in wisdom's ways,
  In the Sabbath school.
DUET—Teachers there with pleasant smile,
    Lead our thoughts to heaven the while,
CHORUS—Tell us Jesus—once a child,
    Cares for such as we.

And they tell us of his love,
  How he left his home above,
Came to earth his grace to prove—
  Died on Calvary.
    Oh, the precious truths we learn,
    May we all to Jesus turn,
    And our hearts within us burn,
    Burn with love divine.

Then shall we, a blood-washed band,
  Teachers and dear children, stand,
In that happy, happy land,
  From the Sabbath school.
    To the Saviour's feet we bring
    Our bright crowns, and then we'll sing,
    And we'll make sweet heaven ring
    With our grateful song.

And the joyful strain shall be,
  Glory, honor, praise to thee,
Father, Son, and Spirit, Three,
  Praise forever more.
    Our glad voices let us raise,
    In a song of love and praise,
    That we're taught in wisdom's ways,
    In the Sabbath school.

PRAISE THE LORD.

[From the Plymouth, page 184.]

Let every heart rejoice and sing,
  Let choral anthems rise;
Ye reverend men and children, bring
  To God your sacrifice:
CHORUS—For he is good; the Lord is good,
    And kind are all his ways;
      With songs and honors sounding loud,
    The Lord Jehovah praise.
      While the rocks and the rills,
    While the vales and the hills,
      A glorious anthem raise,
    Let each prolong the grateful song,
      And the God of our fathers praise,
      And the God of our fathers praise.

He bids the sun to rise and set;
  In heaven his power is known;
And earth, subdued to him, shall yet
  Bow low before his throne.
    For he is good, etc.

HERE AM I.

[From the Evergreen, page 102.]

Listen, 'tis thy Father
  Calling from on high,
As he did to Samuel,
  From the midnight sky.
Answer, meekly answer,
  Father! here am I,
Father! I would hear thee,
Love, obey, revere thee,
Be forever near thee,
  Father, here am I.

Hark! 'tis Jesus speaking,
  Love beams in his eye,
Calling little children,
  Beck'ning infants nigh—
Run to him and answer
  Saviour! here am I.
Jesus, kindly take me,
Thine adopted make me,
Never, Lord! forsake me,
  Saviour! here am I.

List! the Spirit whispers,
  " Wherefore will ye die!"
From his gentle pleading
  Do not, do not fly!
Ere too late, give answer
  Spirit! here am I.
Father, all provide me,
Saviour, keep me, hide me,
Spirit, teach me, guide me—
  Spirit here am I.

LOWELL.

[From the Plymouth, page 33.]

Spread, my soul, thy golden pinions—
  Bask in heaven's celestial ray—
Tis a foretaste of the glories,
  Saved for that eternal day!
When thy pilgrimage is over,
  And the clouds of sin are past,
Then if faithful to thy mission
  Thou shalt reach that goal at last.
CHORUS—As the tide is flowing, flowing,
      Onward to return no more—
    So may heavenly breezes blowing,
      Waft my soul to Canaan's shore!

Though the path be long and dreary,
   And my way by thorns beset;
I will bravely onward journey,
   Hopeful of the blessing yet!
Trusting in a loving Father;
   One whose mighty arm is strong;
I will brave life's surging billows,
   'Till I see the shining throng!—Cho.

Come, then, all who seek God's favor—
   See the open gospel door,
From the highways and the hedges
   Gather in, ye needy poor!
Gather in, and taste the banquet,
   Spread by wondrous love divine;
Then shall all things past and present,
   All in earth and heaven be thine!—Cho.

STAND UP, MY SOUL.

[From the Evergreen, page 108.]

Stand up, my soul! shake off thy fears,
   And gird the gospel armor on;
March to the gates of endless joy,
   Where Jesus, thy great Captain's gone.
Hell and thy sins resist thy course,
   But hell and sin are vanquished foes;
Thy Jesus nailed them to the cross,
   And sung their triumph when he rose.

Then let my soul march boldly on,
   Press forward to the heavenly gate
There peace and joy eternal reigns,
   And glittering robes for conquerors wait.
There shall I wear a starry crown,
   And triumph in Almighty grace;
While all the armies of the skies
   Join in my glorious Leader's praise.

JESUS, WE THY LAMBS WOULD BE.

[From the Sabbath School Bell, No. 2, page 26.]

Jesus, we thy lambs would be,
Humbly we would follow thee,
Waiting for the joyful day,
When all care will pass away,
When the reaping time shall come,
And angels shout the harvest home,
When the reaping time shall come,
And angels' shout the harvest home.

Now the field with grain is white,
Now the day is dawning bright,—
Brighter far the sky will be,
When our Master we shall see,
When the reaping time, etc.

May we wait, and watch and pray,
For the coming of that day,
When the wheat shall sifted be,
And the chaff be driven from thee:
When the reaping time, etc.

AWAKE AND SING THE SONG.

[From the Evergreen, page 27.]

Awake and sing the song
  Of Moses and the Lamb;
Wake every heart and every tongue,
  To praise the Saviour's name,
CHORUS—Sing the song,
      Of Moses and the Lamb,
      Wake every heart and every tongue,
      To praise the Saviour's name.

Sing of his dying love,
　Sing of his rising power;
Sing how he intercedes above
　For those whose sins he bore.

Sing on your heavenly way,
　Ye ransomed sinners sing;
Sing on, rejoicing every day,
　In Christ the eternal King.

AND IS IT TRUE?

[From the Evergreen, page 107.]

And is it true what I am told,
　That there are lambs within the fold
Of God's beloved Son?
　That Jesus Christ, with tender care,
Will in his arms most gently bear
　The helpless "little one."
　The helpless "little one."

And I, a little straying lamb,
　May come to Jesus as I am,
Though merit I have none;
　May now be folded in his breast,
As birds within the parent's nest,
　And be his "little one."
　And be his "little one."

Others there are who love me too:
　But who, with all their love, can do,
What Jesus Christ hath done?
　Then, if he teaches me to pray,
I'll surely go to him, and say,
　Lord, bless thy "little one."
　Lord, bless thy "little one."

I WOULD NOT LIVE ALWAY.

[From the Plymouth, page 186.]

I would not live alway; I ask not to stay,
Where storm after storm rises dark o'er the way,
The few lurid mornings that dawn on us here,
Are enough for life's woes, full enough for its cheer.

I would not live alway thus fettered by sin,
Temptation without, and corruption within;
E'en the rapture of pardon is mingled with fears
And the cup of thanksgiving with penitent tears.

I would not live alway; no, welcome the tomb,
Since Jesus hath lain there, I dread not its gloom;
There, sweet be my rest till he bid me arise,
To hail him in triumph descending the skies.

Who, who would live alway, away from his God,
Away from yon heaven, that blissful abode,
Where the rivers of pleasure flow o'er the bright plains,
And the noontide of glory eternally reigns.

Where the saints of all ages in harmony meet,
Their Saviour and brethren transported to greet,
While the anthems of rapture unceasingly roll,
And the smile of the Lord is the feast of the soul!

INDEX.

www.ingramcontent.com/pod-product-compliance
Lightning Source LLC
Chambersburg PA
CBHW020847270326
41928CB00006B/581